Pathways

to

Inner Peace

Life-saving Processes for Healing
HEART - MIND - SOUL

Rev. James Webb

Pathways to Inner Peace

Published by: Prism Publishing Co.

ISBN: 0-9663277-1-3

Printed in the United States of America

prismpub@aol.com
www.revjimwebb.com
revjimwebb@aol.com

This book is Dedicated to:

Iley and Luvenia Battle

through whom I learned the
truth of Unconditional Love

and to:

Lee Anna Webb

in whom I still see the
reflection of Unconditional Love

Acknowledgments

First of all, I'd like to express my gratitude to Andy Field, whose editing input turned random ideas into readable text.

———

Dave Turner's vision and precision created the perfect photo.

———

Thanks to Carl Poleskey's constant support and Daniel Neusom's constant counsel, I was able to stay true to my dream of offering the gift of my understandings to others.

———

Thanks also to the members and friends of the Takoma Park Metaphysical Chapel, and other friends whose support and encouragement buoyed me, and confirmed that the wisdom contained in this book was needed by others.

———

Finally, thanks to the friends who patiently understood while I had my nose "buried in this book."

Table of Contents

- *The Formation of My "False-Ego"...*
- *The Formation of Your "False-Ego"...*
- *"Root Cause Exercise"...*
- *Assessing Your Self Image...*
- *A Deeper Look at the "False-Ego"...*
- *What Have We Wrought?...*
- *The "False Ego"...*
- *Masking...*
- *Routinizing...*

CONTENTS
. . B . .

CONTENTS
. . C . .

Chapter 5:

(Opening To GOD)

- *A New Understanding of GOD...*
- *Understanding Our Escape Route...*
- *Building A Bridge to GOD...*
- *Prayer Is Talking to GOD,*
     Meditation is Listening to GOD...
- *Prayer and Meditation Will*
     Build Our Escape Route...

Chapter 6:

(A Key Tool On The Journey)

- *Find the Right Space...*
- *Find the Right Time...*
- *Learn to Concentrate...*
- *Free Yourself of External Distractions...*
- *Watch What Happens...*
- *Strengthening Your Meditations...*
- *Unleash Your Imagination...*
- *Create Your "Concentration Scene"...*
- *Mentally Construct Your Safe Space...*
- *Your Safe Space is the Launching Pad for your Journey...*
- *"My Safe Space"...*

CONTENTS
. . D . .

CONTENTS
. . E . .

Preface

IT WOULD REQUIRE an enormous volume to list the countless (and still counting) self-help/psychology books published yearly. It is for this reason that I find *Pathways To Inner Peace* so refreshing, for it transcends this single catagory to encompass the entire realm of human experience. The author himself is also an example of this transcendence, that being an individual who crosses the so-called traditional boundries of social distinction concerning racial, sexual and economic tolerance in America. Yet these highly stressful conditions the author endured became the catalyst for a remarkable transformation of personal consciousness and self-discovery. Not only did Jim Webb discover how to use the power of spirituality to heal his own mind and body, but his ability to translate this process into a clear system of life-saving steps makes his trials and resultant success inspiring and downright essential for humanity. It is difficult to justify complaining about one's chances for raising their station in life after learning of the position Jim was/is faced with daily, but to have also been a victim of violence to top it off makes it almost surreal. Jim's story, if submitted as a Hollywood script, would probably be rejected as too implausable or overly melodramatic. To have 4 strikes against you is difficult enough, but to later actually rise to assume a position of higher authority, where one's life cause is dedicated to offering guidance and healing to others after experiencing this level of personal suffering is simply extraordinary.

As the title implies, this book reveals a series of pathways, which when linked, form a continuous process of healing. Without being scientific or religious in the standard sense as we generally define these terms, the author has successfully developed a hybrid system of techniques based on the integration of science and spirituality, leading to self-transformation. If consistently applied, this approach will allow one to achieve the intended goal of maintaining an ongoing sense of inner peace and healthy physical being. Thus, included in this scenario, is the resultant new evolving psychology and physicality. In essence, putting these exercises into daily practice will dramatically change both mental and physical attributes of the human organism.

Due to this universality, *Pathways To Inner Peace* is meant for everybody. These principles work for everybody. No matter what one's background or lifestyle, freedom from mental conflict, personal healing and living with a deep sense of inner peace is available and works the same for all. Of course many who have felt stigmatized by living the alternative lifestyle may feel more confortable practicing their religious beliefs within the struture of the author's ministry, but no one should mistake this for being strictly a refuge for the misunderstood of society. Rev. Webb has presented a means for connecting with the Godliness within, and so offers a new approach to healing, regardless of one's religious or secular upbringing. He offers *freedom from self-tyranny,* a tyranny originally developed from a limited understanding of the world, a tyranny which continues to support false premises, which later evolved to support the false-ego or self, a false image operating as a defense mechanism to create an externalized version of what one believes society will condone. It is a sad state of affairs when individuals, on a day-to-day basis, believe they must misrepresent themselves based on the premise that their survival depends on it, when in reality, in the end, their self-survival depends on being who they *really are.* We have to love ourselves before we can receive love from others (the only exception being the unconditional love between child and mother in the early stages of growth). To love ourselves, we need to believe that we are worthy of being loved. To believe we are worthy of being loved, we must acknowledge that the creator of the universe loves us. The author emphasizes the point that 'since we exist, as intended by the creator, we are important entites and loved in the universe — that is why we are here and encompass the particular form that we are.

Reading through the table of contents I am impressed by the wonderfully clear encapsulation of the process toward creating well-being. One acknowledges the pain; recognizes the false-ego; learns to see the boundaries of their self-imposed prison; explores their pervading consciousness and comes to a new understanding; learns to use the tools of meditation to discover a safe environment for discovering and accepting truth; mastering the skills for re-aligning the mind and body according to these new found truths; clearing up the emotional blockages interfering with the healthy flow of the system; altering the chemical messages via the pharmaceutical factory in the brain through the use of the power of prayer; and empowering newly formed beliefs to transform one's life to support optimum mental and physical well-being.

As there is no limit to this process, whereby a person's evolution is a never-ending journey of discovery and transformation, the principles presented in this book will never become outdated, just as the eternal basis of who we are will always remain as the creator originally designed us.

Pathways to Inner Peace can be viewed as the 'bible of self-healing' – a companion to all who seek being (not running from) themselves, in which one learns to freely receive the pleasures God endowed us to be able to enjoy in our lives without guilt, fearful expectations, or remorse. This is the amazing, groundbreaking, inspiring, profound, life-changing work which makes *Pathways...* a major contribution to the area of human growth and evolution leading to a healthier present and future for generations to come.

David Zinn
International Media Communications, Inc.
New York / Beverly Hills

Preface

. . vi . .

Foreword

Pathways to Inner Peace can be read in several ways. It can be read with the eyes as if it were an essay with an autobiographical story inside, or it can be read from the heart as a tool that can be used to help you find inner peace and your own spirituality. It can be read from a detached, objective perspective where you simply read the words, or you can consume this book in an interactive way, ingesting the words, participating in the exercises and really taking in the book's major points. It can be read in one sitting or it can be used as an ongoing tool in your pursuit of inner peace. However you choose to use this book, may the light of GOD that shines within you and upon you grow as a result of your reading of this book.

As I was writing this book, I received a very powerful message that may help you. I will share the essence of this message with you here:

Do not be afraid of this process
▲ ▲ ▲ ▲ ▲ ▲ ▲

There is no reason for you to have any fear, knowing that you are loved, protected, and were created by the grand master of the universe. You are currently feeling fear because you are about to embark on one of the biggest adventures of your life – the beginning of your path to your own inner power. You have personally witnessed many of the human experiences that were designed to heal you and move you into the realm of the divine – the Kingdom of Heaven, which is on earth. The Kingdom of Heaven is created with your consciousness as you heal your mind and your life. Now you are focusing on the part of your journey where you experience your spiritual nature. Let the light and love of GOD caress you through this process. You will find this experience to be quite pleasurable, because as you work with this book, you will be continually bathed in the light of GOD, for this light is open to you any time you make yourself available to it.

FOOTPRINTS IN THE SAND

One night I was walking along the beach.

Many scenes from my life flashed across the sky.

In each scene I noticed footprints in the sand.

Sometimes there were two sets of footprints.

Sometimes there was one set of footprints.

This bothered me because I noticed that during the low periods of my life,

When I was suffering from anguish, sorrow, or defeat,

I could see only one set of footprints.

So I said to the Lord,

"You promised me, Lord, that you would walk with me always.

But I noticed that during the most trying periods of my life

There has been only one set of footprints in the sand.

Why when I have needed you most, have you not been there for me?"

The lord replied "The times when you have seen only one set of footprints

Is when I carried you."

~ Mary Stevenson

Pathways to Inner Peace

. . 2 . .

Chapter One

PAIN

A Catalyst for the Journey

Are you aware that every painful experience you ever had has been an opportunity to experience your spirituality? Do you know that each and every painful experience a person has is a "wake-up call" to the fact that not only are you a physical being, but also a spiritual one? Did you ever notice that most people cry out to GOD in times of crisis or suffering?

As a minister who reached thousands and counseled hundreds of people over the years, the most common question asked is: "How do I heal my emotions and reach this elusive state of inner peace?" In response to this question, I simply had to look no futher than my own experiences of personal transformation and the wisdom and insights that I gained from this process. Finally, I realized that through my experiences, I had constructed a path that will, if properly applied, lead to inner peace and personal transformation in all aspects of life. However, this journey began at one of my low points. I wrote the following words at one of the most painful perods in my life, and in writing this passage, I came to a deeper awareness of GOD's presence in my life. You may identify with some of the emotions that are expressed in the passage, because I'm sure that you have been in a similar place at one point or another. At the time, it may not have seemed like a day at the beach, but it probably began an important process for you — the process of Opening to GOD.

Mother, Father, GOD. I open to your light and love at this time because there is nothing else that I can do. I feel such deep pain — such searing pain — such relentless pain. It shoots through my psyche like a bullet and rips my heart open. It scars my soul. I can only scream because the pain is so great. This pain is lodged in the caverns of my mind and is indelibly etched into my soul. It has been there for eons. As I write this I can only touch the borders of this intense pain. It is so hot that it sears my skin. It is so deep that I feel that I shall never escape it. It is so all encompassing that it smothers me. It is so heavy that it crushes me. It has compounded — layer after layer after layer. Each passing day brings me even more pain. This world is too painful for my survival.

What can I do to dull the pain? What can I do to escape the intense pressure of the pain? What can I do? What can I possibly do? I feel the lashes of a million whips. I feel the pricks of a million pins. I feel the sting of a million hornets. I feel the searing pain of a million branding irons. I feel the pain of a being whose very core has suffered eons of negation, destruction, annihilation, rejection, denigration abuse, separation, and hell. Hell is my time on earth.

I feel the deep despair of one who has no hope. I feel the pain of a child abandoned by its father. I feel the pain of a child rejected by its peers. I feel the pain of a child ridiculed by others. I feel the pain of a child neglected by its caretakers. I feel the pain of a teen who feels no love, no life, no connection and no belonging. If feel the pain of a teenager who doesn't fit. I feel the pain of a being that is hopelessly, irreparably and fatally flawed. I feel that my time on earth is a death sentence waiting to happen. I feel a slow, lingering pending death. I feel the pain of a teenager that has a defect. I feel the pain of a teenager who has many defects. I feel the pain of a teenager who is abused. I feel the pain of a teenager who hates himself, but who is not yet aware of the depth of his self-hatred. I feel the pain of a young adult who does not belong. I feel the pain of a young adult who does not fit. I feel the pain of an adult at a crossroads. Do I choose life, or do I choose death. What awaits me in death? Will the calm of death mitigate the pain of life?

Shall I endure? Shall I turn to drugs? Drugs will certainly dull the pain. Sex will temporarily take my attention away from the pain. Food will temporarily ease the pain. Gambling will cancel out the pain by replacing it with a temporary high.

Shall I deny the pain? Shall I let the pain collect in the recesses of my body as it collects in the re-

cesses of my mind — causing blockages, diseases, cancers, and other physical manifestations?
Or shall I surrender the pain to you?

How did I get to this emotional abyss? First of all, let me explain to you who I am. I am a black gay man who grew up poor in America and a victim of abuse.

That says a lot. Most of what it says is that my life hasn't been easy. I could be a poster boy for victimhood. I grew up black in a race based society. I grew up poor in a society that values money. I grew up gay in a society that values machismo. In other words I grew up feeling (in a deep, deep way) that I was fatally flawed and had no value.

This identity (which you might rightfully infer has been a challenge) has brought me many experiences. Some of them have been extremely painful. These painful experiences, however, have forced me to search for a new reality, for inner peace, a new reason for being, and ultimately a new identity not based on pain, but on truth.

My search led me through many experiences that caused me to question my life and the very nature of GOD. Through my explorations, I discovered many truths about myself, the world and GOD. These discoveries led me to a place of bliss and inner peace that most people find difficult to even imagine. As a result, I constructed a path to inner peace that can be successfully applied by anyone (regardless of their background or experiences), leading them to their own path to inner peace. This path consists of exercises, meditations, prayers and other tools for re-discovering and deepening the spirituality that is the living essence, the life force and creative energy of humanity. I will now share these tools with you, as well as walk you through each step, together forming a process of healing leading to that higher state of inner awareness and personal peace.

Pathways to Inner Peace

Chapter Two

THE FALSE EGO

Survival Kit of the Soul

My search for inner peace began shortly after my 13th Birthday, when I was beaten, kicked and stomped into an unconscious state. As I lay hospitalized, I pondered my life and what would happen with it. I vowed to improve it. As a result, I became enamored with the self-help books that were popular in the seventies (e.g. Your Erroneous Zones, I'm O.K., You're O.K., The Power of Positive Thinking). This interest was matched by an interest in the occult (Edgar Cayce — The Sleeping Prophet, Many Mansions, and anything by Ruth Montgomery). You see, before the "new age" these books were in a section of the library called "The Occult."

Over the last 20 years, several things have happened: "The Occult" section of the library transformed into the New Age section; and the Self-Help section of the library transformed into the Self-Empowerment section. Little did I know that these two seemingly diverse fields of exploration would merge in an interesting way to help me in my transformation into manhood.

I had no idea that the work I did with myself (as a result of the self-help movement) and the spiritual insights that I gained (as a result of my exploration into the world of metaphysics) would dovetail later in life. Those concepts that I comprehended "intellectually" would eventually be understood at a deeper level of my consciousness (in other words, the intellectual understandings that I gathered in my head, would eventually move into my heart, as I assimilated them in a deeper way through my experiences). At that time, they simply seemed like practical tools to help me through a very rocky time in my life.

Through my experiences, I developed a deep understanding of (and an empathy for) the pain many people feel. Because my reality was so painful, I was forced to contemplate and find a less painful reality. Due to the painful experiences in my life, I was forced to find and utilize the necessary tools I had discovered to create a less painful reality, through a deeper connection with my spirituality and a rigorous program of emotional healing. By mastering the means for entering and maintaining this new reality instead of what would have been a self-defeating and painful existence based on my crippling past, to reach a point of inner peace, financial prosperity, professional success, and joy that most of us only dream about, I had to go through this process of self-healing. I wrote this book in order to share this path of healing with others, so that you can re-discover the means for breaking free of the prison constructed from your own self-induced pain.

The False Ego

The Formation of My False-Ego

My perceptions and my beliefs about myself were shaped by my interpretations of my experiences. They were also perpetuated by the popular culture and the media. Unfortunately they were also perpetuated by me.

Some of my earlier experiences include an incident when I was in the first grade. I was running across the street with a young Caucasian girl named Jamie. We were racing and she fell and skinned her knee. Apparently she went home and told her mother that I pushed her down, and the next day I received a very vicious spanking from the first grade teacher. I couldn't understand why the beating was so vicious and somehow, subconsciously, it occurred to me that there was immense anger, because this was a little white girl, and I was a little black boy.

I also remember the first time that I began to believe that I was ugly. It was after I got glasses in the second grade, and all of a sudden I didn't feel attractive. Perhaps that old cliché "Boys don't make passes at girls who wear glasses" had slipped into my consciousness. I had just gotten glasses and believed that glasses were somewhat clumsy and unattractive. Every year we had pictures taken in school, and that year I remember taking home my pictures and crumbling them because I felt that I was ugly. That was when I first became aware of a shame within me. That was when I first began to hate myself.

The shame continued because I was poor and black. I remember the shame of having to go to the store with Food Stamps. I remember how humiliating that was and how low that made me feel. I remember the pain of not having all the things that the other children had. I didn't have the same clothes, I didn't have the same toys, and I didn't seem to have a father. The confusion about my parental situation sticks in my mind because I really missed that guidance. My mother had divorced from my father early in my life. I came to know my mother's boyfriend as my father, and after a while it became clear that my mother's boyfriend was my biological father (even though I was named after the man she had married). I remember being very confused by this truth, but being more bewildered because neither of these men were around much and neither seemed to be dependable. Being without this male support and guidance made me feel less than human, less than full, less than loved. I envied the children who had fathers who cared about them. Somehow I felt less valuable because I did not have a father.

My pain continued through my elementary school years, as the other children began to pick on me. You see, I was very intelligent, but I was in an environment that did not value intelligence. I was considered effeminate and weak. And I believe subconsciously that the other children picked up on that fact, and started calling me names, laughing at me, and ridiculing me. The pain that this caused me seared my psyche in a very deep way.

I remember the first time I was jealous of another child. I was about four or five, and one of the neighborhood children had a red fire engine. He also had a father and a stable family unit unlike my situation. I was jealous and I hated myself because I did not have what this child had. I took out that anger on the other child. I tried to take away his red fire engine. As he was taller and stronger, he proceeded to beat the hell out of me.

This pattern of behavior would continue throughout my life. My anger at myself, my self-hatred, and the pain I felt as a result of my situation, would turn inward and outward, and manifest in many future situations that were in essence caused by this deep level of self-loathing.

My confusion continued through the bewildering time of adolescence. In early adolescence I was beaten unconscious by another young man, over a minor dispute. I was hospitalized for several days. My depression over this event lasted a full year. I was angry with myself and the world (depression is simply anger turned inward). I felt somehow that this beating was not simply the result of me being picked on and despised by other children because I was perceived as being weak. It also seemed to be linked to my feelings of guilt regarding my burgeoning sexuality, which I knew at that time was a primarily homosexual orientation.

The beating, the denigration through my childhood, the shame I felt for being black, the shame I felt for being poor, the shame I felt for being gay, led me to constructing layer upon layer of self-hatred, creating a pyramid of self-loathing. This self-hatred magnified the fears and uncertainties that I carried with me. However, this self-hatred was not readily apparent to me or to others. It was a deeply internalized feeling that only bubbled to the surface occasionally.

Of course I did everything I could to hide it, to ignore it, to deny it. I developed a "public face" — a mask so that people wouldn't see the "real" me. I overcompensated academically by being an over-achiever. I overcompensated socially by developing a warm and winning personality. I overcompensated physically by working on my body. I overcompensated materially by pursuing wealth.

In addition, I found the self-help movement of the seventies as an outlet. You recall some of the books such as 'I'm Okay, You're Okay.' or 'Your Erroneous Zones.' Books like these gave me a new intellectual framework for loving and accepting myself on the surface. This interest was matched by an interest in spiritual and psychic phenomena. This was of course before the New Age movement began. And over the years, through the work that I have discovered and personally applied to myself, I have constructed a path of healing that you too can use. This path takes the information that is intellectually sound and logical, and helps us to use this knowledge not only on an intellectual plane but to assimilate the ideas deeply within our heart center. You may already be familiar with many aspects of this path in your mind. However, it has been said that the longest journey is the journey from the head to the heart. This is a journey that takes intellectual understandings and transforms them into a deep, intensive "knowing" that you feel as an integral part of you. This path opens your heart and connects your heart with your greater being, and in doing so, helps you to forge a strong connection with a divine and infinite power that has always been available to you. This path is a journey to the Heart of GOD, which is the space of complete and unconditional love.

You may ask "what does your journey have to do with me? I am not black, I am not gay, I was not born poor, I did not suffer your injustices." My journey is relevant because we all are shaped by our experiences. Although the specific experience may not be identical, we can all probably remember times when we felt shamed, unworthy and less than whole. We can all probably remember when our experiences said we were not good enough! Think of some of your life's pivotal moments. Then ask yourself HOW they shaped your concept of yourself. Did they affirm you or did they denigrate you? Then ask how these experiences changed how you think of yourself now? Examine not only what you think of yourself on the surface, but what you think of yourself, deep down inside.

The Formation of Your False-Ego

Our experiences play an enormous role in shaping our self image. However, that image has probably also been shaped by the media. Co-dependent love songs offer a sterling example: Whitney Houston — 'I Am Nothing, Nothing, Nothing, If I Don't Have You.' Diana Ross and The Supremes — 'My World Is Empty Without You Babe' are two that come to mind.

Let's look at the media again more closely. The media tells us that we are less than perfect and less than whole if we have bad breath, or bad teeth. The media tells us we are undesirable if we are without the latest clothes, the perfect diction, classic good looks or the "right" social background. During the course of thirty odd years you've probably received millions of impressions, if not billions along this line. Some are so subtle that they are imperceptible. However, these impressions have lodged in your conscious mind – and in your subconscious mind. Many tell you in a very subtle and sometimes in a very obvious way that you are not good enough. The lyrics of Mick Jagger's 'Beast of Burden,' come to mind. These lyrics said: Am I strong enough? Am I tough enough? Am I rich enough?

With these examples we see how advertising warps our self image and deflates our ability to love ourselves. Unfortunately, we also do it to ourselves, and the way I will explain HOW it has been perpetuated by us is the BIG LIE. Let's start examining how we perpetuate our own negative self-image by examining the concept of a lie. If you tell a lie the first time it's a lie. If you tell a lie the second time it's still a lie. The third time the lie is stated, you start to embellish it. When you tell the lie the fourth time you embellish it even more with additional descriptive details. It becomes a hydra-headed monster. When you tell a lie the fifth time it is no longer a lie, it becomes a story. By the tenth time you've told that lie, your mind believes that the lie is the truth. Your perception has shifted and you believe that the event has truly happened. By the same token the messages that we have received from the media, from the popular culture, from our peers and from our families have been repeated and repeated and repeated. In our minds we take those messages as gospel. Let's call the amalgamation of these messages the popular consciousness.

I, of course heard, in many, many ways; many, many times how worthless, how disgusting, how contemptible, FAGS were. You can't miss the "subtle" innuendo that BLACKS are worthless, lazy and stupid. Interestingly enough it hasn't been the obvious things that have pained me and made me feel less than human. It's easy to dismiss the obvious as simple ignorance. More often its insidiously subtle:

⚜ Hearing the click of a car door when I walk past a car—

⚜ Seeing a woman subconsciously clutch her purse as I approached (even when the woman was a real estate agent trying to sell me a $300,000 house!) —

⚜ Hearing a co-worker or an academic colleague ask me a question, hear me give the answer and then ask another colleague to verify the answer —

Subconsciously they believe that I can't have the intelligence or vision or wherewithal to answer the question correctly because, somehow, that would threaten their self-esteem. In college a colleague was amazed because he heard an African-American explaining a concept to others, and was stunned because the other people were listening and actually respected this person. His perception was that Blacks did not deserve respect, and he was surprised when they received it. I know first hand, the humiliation of having a security guard follow me around a "high end" store. The degradation of being stopped by the police for no apparent reason because I drive an expensive car in an affluent neighborhood is still fresh in my mind because it still occurs. Recently a policeman didn't even feign a bogus reason for stopping me — he simply asked "is this car stolen?"

My situation however is not unique to me or any human being. I have only shaved the tip of the iceberg of my experiences in offering examples of the frequent denigration, the de-humanization we all experience during the course of our lives. This de-humanization has made us feel unworthy, separate and unequal. These experiences formed our "false-ego."

The "false-ego" is a term used to describe the "outward" characteristics that describe you. These descriptors usually include dimensions such as your age, race, gender, sexuality, socio-economic positioning and your life experiences. The false ego can also be known as the "personality," or your "name, rank and serial number." The false ego gets its sense of self worth from the "outer" trappings, and needs other people to say "hey, you're o.k." The false ego often takes over your consciousness. The false ego has also evolved in order to ensure survival on earth. It began evolving and forming from birth, and continues to evolve through the experiences that we have throughout our lives.

For example, one person I know vividly remembers the first time he experienced guilt and shame regarding his sexuality. As an innocent, perfect and playful child, he and his male friend were "massaging" each other and it felt good. Later that afternoon, when he went home, he innocently mentioned to his mother that he and "John-John" massaged each other. He still remembers his mother's face becoming contorted with rage and disgust, and he remembers his mother's vitriolic and almost violent reaction. As a child, this person believed that his mother was the center of his universe and would have done almost anything to please her. Subconsciously he believed that she had the power of "life and death" over him, and did not want to risk her wrath. As a result of his admonition, he received the message loud and clear that receiving pleasure from the touch of another man was deeply, terribly wrong, and experienced a deep, and lasting shame that he buried deeply into his subconscious mind. This experience was so scarring, that it remained locked in his subconscious mind for almost 30 years. Only now is he finally strong enough to deal with the deeply internalized shame and self-loathing that came as a result of this experience.

If you look back on your experiences, I'm sure you will remember feeling less than worthy and less than whole. They may be major experiences such as the one described above, or they may be minor experiences that you have forgotten about. Take a minute now. Look at your own life and look at these situations. Look at them objectively, for you are now taking the first giant steps in your Journey to the Inner Peace.

To help you, I have designed a meditation that you may use. You may choose to record this meditation in your own voice, and listen to it as you go deeper, into a place of healing. You may use this meditation as you go further on your Journey to Inner Peace.

If you are reading this book you probably don't need to be convinced to do these exercises. By buying this book, you are motivated to improve. The first step is: identify how and why you feel less than total inner peace. The following exercise will help you identify the root causes of your sources of discontent.

Root Cause Exercise

As we enter this meditation, we begin by becoming aware of our breath.

❧ We INHALE deeply — As we inhale, we think about the concept of peace.

❧ We EXHALE deeply — exhaling the stresses of the day.

❧ Once again we INHALE deeply breathing in peace. As we breathe in, we concentrate on the concept of peace. We think about what images represent peace to us, and we concentrate on those images. We think about what feeling overtakes us as we think about peace, and we concentrate on those feelings.

❧ We EXHALE deeply relieving the stresses of the day.

❧ And again we INHALE deeply breathing in peace.

❧ One final time we EXHALE deeply, releasing the pressures of the day.

❧ As you continue to breathe, with every breath you become more relaxed. With every breath you become more at peace.

❧ With every breath you become more at one with all that is around you.

❧ With every breath you breathe in more contentment.

❧ With every breath you breathe in more peace.

❧ With every breath you breathe in more love. And as you continue breathing, you feel a Golden-Pink Light surrounding your head. You feel this Light surrounding your head and relaxing the top of your head. You feel this light moving down, around your facial muscles. You feel this light moving down to the base of your neck. You feel this light relaxing the muscles at the base of your neck, relaxing your facial muscles, and you feel this Golden-Pink beautiful light surrounding your throat.

❧ It surrounds your throat and your neck, and relaxes your throat and your neck.

❧ You feel this beautiful Golden-Pink light, surrounding your shoulders, which begin to droop as they relax.

❧ Your shoulders relax and they begin to droop and you feel this Golden-Pink light moving down your arms.

❧ Relaxing your arm muscles, relaxing the tension within your hands, you continue to feel this relaxation moving down your torso, moving past your heart and your internal organs and they all begin to relax.

✤ Your organs now begin to flow with a more natural rhythm of peace.

✤ And you feel this Golden-Pink light moving down into your reproductive organs, moving down into your buttocks, and moving down past the base of your spine, down the legs, past your knees, down your calves, down your feet, to the tip of your toes.

✤ And you feel this Golden - Pink light now surrounding you in this cocoon of relaxation.

✤ In this cocoon of relaxation you are protected.

✤ In this cocoon of relaxation you are whole.

✤ In this cocoon of relaxation you are loved.

✤ In this space your mind is open and flexible. In this space your mind is at peace, and flexible. It is this space where your mind works and moves backward. It moves backward in time.

✤ Your mind moves backward in time. It moves backward to a place where you have had trauma.

✤ Your mind moves backward to a place where you

developed "key" concepts about yourself that were not affirming to you.

❦ You move back to the situation and you ask, "Let me see the *key* events that have caused me to form the opinion of myself, that I now hold."

❦ "Help me to see how I have formed the opinion of myself that I have." And as you think these words, your mind moves back to the first experience that you had that formed your self image.

❦ And your mind slowly, slowly, moves forward, to additional scenes in your life where your perception of yourself was formed.

❦ Your mind continues to move forward from scene to scene of how your perception of yourself was formed.

❦ Your mind moves slowly from scene to scene, and you make a note of each scene where you developed a *key* image of yourself.

❦ A *key* indicator of how you feel about yourself.

❦ You continue to make a note of these *key* scenes, and your mind continues to move forward.

❦ Your mind moves forward, your mind moves forward,

back to the Here and Now.

And now you have a *key* view of how you formed your "self image."

❧ ❧ ❧

Now that you have finished this exercise, you may want to ask yourself "How Do I Feel?" Many events popped into your mind. Ask yourself "were these experiences loving and affirming or were they painful and traumatic?" Also ask "were they large, life-changing experiences or were they small innocuous scenes. Did someone intentionally harm you, or did someone take an action that inadvertently harmed you?"

Based on this exercise, and your current thought processes, you can start objectively assessing your self image. Through this assessment, you can examine where it helps you and where it harms you. This assessment is critical in moving you to a place where you have only a positive image of yourself based not on others' opinions of you, or your experiences from the past, but based only on GOD's unconditional love for you.

Assessing Your Self-image

At this time, take a moment and jot down as many descriptors as you can think of to describe yourself on the following page:

The False Ego
. . 25 . .

SAMPLE DESCRIPTORS TO DESCRIBE YOURSELF

✳ I am a loving mother ✳

✳ I am a responsible breadwinner ✳

✳ I am a good child ✳

✳ I am professionally competent ✳

Congratulations! Completing this exercise takes a great deal of courage and objectivity. With that same objectivity, let's look back at the descriptors that you used. Let's see if we can identify those descriptors that are based on someone's or something's (like an institution) perception of us.

A Deeper Look at the False-Ego

What you may have found is that many of these descriptors were based on someone's perception of you (based on their judgment and their values). They are probably seeing (and judging) the outer "shell" that you show the world, and evaluating you on some mythical standards of perfection. They are probably judging you based on your "false-ego."

Again, the "false-ego" is a term used to describe the "outward" characteristics that describe you. These descriptors usually include dimensions such as your age, race, gender, sexuality, how much you make, your life experiences and so on. The false ego can also be known as the "personality," or your "name, rank and serial number." The false ego gets its sense of self-worth from the "outer" trappings, and seeks approval from others. The false ego begins to pervade every part of your consciousness. It has also evolved to ensure our survival on the planet. It began evolving and forming from birth, and continues to evolve through the experiences that we have throughout our lives. Let's now take a closer look at how this process occurs.

The "false-ego" can be a trap that keeps us in pain. We may inadvertently believe that our well-being and our sense of self is entirely dependent on the trappings of the "false-ego," and the fear that these "trappings of the ego" could be taken away from us causes much anxiety, fear and grief. For example, part of our definition of ourselves may be that we are a "good" mother. Being a "good" mother, however, is dependent on the conduct of our children, for we believe that "THEY" are judging our children's conduct and finding our parenting skills lacking. As a result, some element of our self worth is derived from (and dependent on) our children's conduct (which we cannot always control). As a result, we have an overriding sense of shame when our child misbehaves at the mall, and we would do anything to maintain our sense of self-worth (including physically harming the child) to control the child's behavior in order to assuage our false ego.

Another example might be that we see ourselves as the "breadwinner" and judge ourselves as lovable based on how well we fill that role. The fear that we will not adequately fulfill that role may start to permeate our professional behavior and cause us to behave callously at best, and unethically at worst, to the point where we would do "anything" to get ahead. As this behavior manifests, we are constantly in fear that we will not have what we need to fulfill the role of "breadwinner" to the satisfaction of our "false-ego" self, and this fear causes us (and others) pain.

To understand the "false-ego" more fully, let's look more closely at how it evolved. When we are born, we receive all that we need to survive from our parents. If something is withheld, we believe we will not survive, therefore we are totally dependent on our parents. Through this process, we have shifted our perception. We believe that our parents are the source of all that we need to survive, and we have shift-ed our perception from the truth that GOD is the source and that our parents are simply the "conduits" of GOD's suste-nance. We have substituted the illusion of the parents being the source, for the truth of GOD as the source. This "substi-tution" continues as we grow. As we become more indepen-dent, we transfer this "substitution" by placing "burden of responsibility" onto peer groups, because we believe that they will give us the love that we need to sustain ourselves. As we evolve further, we transfer this "substitution" onto outer trappings that we believe are the sources of our well-being, such as our jobs, salaries, titles and the trappings of our adult lives.

In addition, we transfer this "substitution" onto our spouses or our dates, who we subconsciously perceive as our surrogate parents. We misperceive that these others hold the same power over us that our parents did (the power of life and death, because we misperceive that they have what we need to survive). As a result, we create hellish situations for ourselves out of the fear that what we need to survive will be taken from us. We construct a "false-ego" as the mechanism that ensures that we always get what we need to survive. The "false ego" also creates the dramas that occur in our lives, from "tug of war" romances to the deep anxiety that we may feel in many situations.

Some examples of the pain and suffering that the false ego include are situations that are familiar to all of us. Have you ever met someone who said they would call you, and then sat at home waiting for the phone to ring? The fear, doubt and anxiety that results is based on the false ego, which needs that call like oxygen in order to feel worthy. And when we "get" a relationship, we will do anything to maintain it (including betraying our own needs and desires) because the relationship becomes our source of validation.

In many cases, the "false ego" fuels our pain and suffering at the workplace too. Our job (or the way someone treats us on it) becomes a source of validation, and when we don't get the respect, recognition or advantages that we think we deserve, we go into a tailspin, because at a deeper level, we think we are unworthy unless things go our way. As a result, we feel that something we need to survive will elude us, and a subtle desperation drives us to commit acts that defy rationality.

We will discuss the concept of the "false-ego" more fully as we continue our Journey to Inner Peace. For now, don't judge the mental and emotional crutches we developed, for we created what we felt we would need to survive. In other words, let's look at the "false-ego" as the Survival Kit for the Soul, because we felt that we needed it. As we expand our consciousness, however, we may understand that part of what the "false-ego" built was based on an illusion, and that illusion now causes us enough discomfort to remove damaging misperceptions and to find inner peace. We now move toward that inner peace through the introspection necessary to give us insights into the illusions that we created. On our Journey to Inner Peace, we move past illusions that no longer serve us.

So how do we begin to attain this new state of being? First of all, we have to become aware of what we have already created, and eliminate what we no longer want. Eliminate the negative, and positive events have room to rush in. We must also understand that we have developed very strong coping skills that are designed to protect us from negative outcomes. However, these coping skills often reinforce our belief in these negative outcomes, and therefore gives them more power to be created. Many of us believe that the world is a very hostile place. As a result, we learn fear, reinforce fear, and create experiences that make us fearful. These coping skills are based on a world that teaches us separation and strife — so we create exactly what we don't want.

So let's look at some of the coping skills that may help create pain and suffering.

Masking

As children, we are innocent and we are perfect. All we want to do is play, explore, create, and be the little magnificent creatures we were meant to be. Little by little we get shamed. Our parents call us bad boys or bad girls. That cramps our style and we stop sensing, expressing and being

the wonderful beings we are. So we put on a mask because we learn what is "acceptable," — acceptable to others, that is. We learn to hide our true selves.

The most perfect example of masking is the behavior that we exhibit in intimate relationships. On the first few dates, we are on our best behavior. Many times we do a helluva good impersonation of our favorite movie star. In truth, we are pulling a "bait and switch" by trying to lure the other person under false pretenses just like our local used car dealer. This works for a while. However, when we find that the other person is getting too close, (perhaps close enough to see the "real" person that lives behind the mask) we pick a fight to put some distance between us. For some reason we were convinced that the other person couldn't love the real us, so we chose some trivial reason to pick a fight and blow the situation all out of proportion. Although you may not be aware of the subconscious motivation, I'm sure you can recall a situation where this happened.

Routinizing

The next thing that we tend to do is routinizing. Routinizing is going through the motions but losing touch with your emotions. Routinizing is losing the awareness of our inner feelings. Routinizing is going through life without ever giving a thought to what it means, or how we really feel. A popular song has the lyric "I am a stranger in my own life," which nails "routinizing" on the head. Routinizing disconnects us from our heart energy, and ultimately leads to a pretty barren existence. Routinizing places us in the ranks of the "walking wounded" — those who have become so emotionally bankrupt that they are unaware of any possibility for lasting peace or bliss in their lives.

Intellectualizing

Intellectualizing is keeping everything in our heads and not letting it travel down to our hearts, where we FEEL it. Intellectualizing involves applying logic and intelligence to situations, and hiding from or denying the emotions involved. A perfect example of this happened to me in 1990. I ended a relationship that had become extremely troublesome. It was clearly one of the most traumatic events in my life. At that time the relationship seemed like the life force, and I had somehow given this relationship an immense amount of power over me. Ending it was almost like ending my life. Regardless, I ended it intellectually in January. And intellectually everything made sense, but I was so busy with other things in my life that I did not let myself at that point FEEL anything. I had much, much, work to do. And so, from January through April it just never occurred to me to feel it. Intellectually the relationship had to end, and so it physically ended. We went through many of the motions of the separation, including consulting attorneys. We went through the motions of the physical separation and we started living our separate lives.

By April fifteenth, which is tax day, I was doing my taxes frantically and running them out to the post office at eleven-twenty p.m. so they could be postmarked by midnight. At midnight, when I returned, the pressure of all the activities leading to April 15th had suddenly lifted from my shoulders. All of a sudden I found myself alone in my house. And all of a sudden I had let down my defenses, perhaps because of fatigue, perhaps because of overwork, perhaps because of the relief that was actually necessary because of the amount of energy I had just expended. But I let down my defenses, and all of a sudden I looked around at the empty house and realized the person with whom I was involved was no longer there. The loss just hit me and I had one of the most violent and cathartic cries that I have ever had. Suddenly everything that was in my head, hit my heart. And it only did so when I let down my defenses and my coping mechanisms. Intellectualizing is keeping things in the head instead of the heart.

Deflecting and Denial

Deflecting is another tactic that is used wonderfully well. Deflecting involves focusing on other peoples issues, and not focusing on our own. We're so busy fixing and diagnosing someone else's issues that we don't focus on ourselves. Deflecting is a type of denial that keeps us from looking into our own dark secret closets and finding the scary monsters within. Denial is a form of selective perception that is very strong. We filter out information that would force us to confront ourselves. It can be so strong that I have observed two people perceiving the same words in totally different ways.

I vividly recall seeing a dear friend who had been out of town for a 12 month assignment. I hadn't seen him in a while, and he had noticeably lost a tremendous amount of weight. During the course of our conversation, I kept steering the conversation to running, athletics and the benefits of aerobic exercise (assuming that he had adopted aerobics as his new religion based on his weight loss). I didn't perceive his hesitation each time I brought up the subject. By this time, I had seen hundreds (if not thousands) of people get sick and die from AIDS, and could spot the signs of AIDS on a stranger from 100 feet away. However, I assumed my friend had simply started running and doing aerobic exercises, and this accounted for his rapid weight loss. Several weeks after this meeting, he became gravely ill, and he told me that he had AIDS. I was dumbfounded! At that moment, it all made sense, his rapid weight loss, and his hesitation. I also realized that several times over the previous 2 years, he had tried to tell me that he had AIDS, but I valiantly refused to hear what he was trying to tell me. So strong is the power of denial.

Exploring the Hidden Heart

What you may want to do now, is take a moment, go into a semi-meditative state and recognize how you've used any of these techniques that I've described. So surround yourself with wonderful, beautiful light. Feel yourself relax. Feel the light come from the soles of your feet to the top of your head. Feel every muscle in your body relax. Go through each step of the process. Start with relaxing your feet, continue by relaxing your legs, continue by relaxing your thighs, continuing by relaxing your buttocks and sexual organs. Continue to relax your torso, your chest, your shoulders, your arms, your hands. Continue by feeling the light of relaxation climbing up your shoulders. The light continues up your shoulders to relax your throat, the base of your neck. Your facial muscles begin to relax, the crown of your head begins to relax and you surround yourself with White Light. With the White Light of Intelligence you gain insights into how you have used each of these situations. And in this state of peace, of comfort, of bliss, of support, you write them down. No one sees this but you. No one judges you. You just want to attain an awareness of how you've used these techniques to cope. Soon as we come to the here and now, we understand that we do not blame ourselves for the tools that we've used to survive. We just accept this part of ourselves as simply another part that is lovable.

Then we begin to forgive ourselves for any actions that we have taken that have kept us from our hearts. We begin to forgive ourselves by opening to the concept of forgiveness. The concept of forgiveness, is the concept of being willing to see events differently. We now see these events as necessary for us. They were necessary for our survival. Anytime we masked our true feelings. Anytime we shielded our heart. Anytime we deflected or denied our true feelings. Anytime we held things inside. It was what was necessary for our survival. Just as we begun forgiving others for doing things to us, we begin to forgive ourselves. We understand that we did the best we could with what we knew then. And now we are accessing new information, so, we can do the best we can with the new information that we now have.

What Has The Hidden Heart Caused?

So with that forgiveness we move forward and look at everything that the hidden heart has caused us. And we can look at it more objectively for we no longer blame ourselves; we now forgive ourselves.

What has the hidden heart caused? It has caused plenty of dramas in our lives. I can certainly tell you that in my life it has caused much trauma, pain, anger, and rage. And it has caused many conflicts in our lives. I know in my life there was a time when I was always in conflict with someone. It seemed like every time I blinked I was having a fight with co-workers, friends or relatives. Every time I blinked I disliked someone or I was taking offense at someone for some slight, either real or imagined. What I eventually realized was that I was truly mad at myself. These people and their energy was reflecting my own consciousness and the truth that I was mad at myself because I didn't like myself. I didn't like myself because the dominant consciousness told me that I was unlovable. I didn't accept myself because the dominant consciousness told me that I was unacceptable. I didn't nurture myself because the dominant consciousness and the circumstances that had been created told me that I was undeserving. I held a lot of this in through denial. I held a lot of it in through over-achieving. I over-achieved thinking that if I was the perfect student, wore the perfect outward mask, and had the perfect personality, then people would love me and I would therefore become lovable from inside and feel better about myself. I believed that if I had the perfect car, the perfect house, the perfect career, and the perfect endless circle of friends, then I would be acceptable.

The Hidden Heart May Create a "Big Bang!"

What I was doing was hiding my true self, and hiding my heart. I'd built a volcano of unexpressed emotions that was waiting to erupt. This volcano was seething with unregistered and unrecognized pain, fear and negation. It was ready to explode. In my case the hidden heart drew situations to me that caused a big bang. This is the case with others as well. Some of the examples of big bangs are divorce, the death of a loved one, the loss of a job, illness, or even death. These things that are jarring are naturally disruptive, and are drawn to us magnetically as a culmination of many events. These events may seem painful, they may seem trying, but they are truly a new chance for us to open our hearts. They are our wake-up calls. What we find is that many times only in life-threatening (or perceived life-threatening) or painful situations, do we open to GOD and take action. We can get through the daily pain of going to work, and coming home, and living among the walking wounded. We can easily mask and shield and survive, but when we feel our survival is threatened, we then cry out to the higher power.

It is then that we open to The Higher Power's influence in our lives and open to it's healing capabilities. We must realize that we have created this as an opportunity to grow and a chance to heal. So, we have these big bangs. These big bangs tend to shake up the structure or foundation of our lives, which give us an opportunity to question every aspect of our lives. We then open to a new level of truth.

My big bang was the break up I referred to earlier. It made me question every assumption about myself. Prior to this break up I thought that everything was fine. My spiritual understandings were all in my head. None were in my heart. Through this break-up I realized that I had depended on this person in a very subtle and unconscious way for my feeling of self worth. I felt that this other person completed me. He was a big strong man, where I perceived myself as a weak child. He was very successful in business and in the world, where I perceived myself as still forging my success in the world. This man represented to me the father's love that I thought I never had. I thought if I could have and keep his love, I would be lovable. My inner child felt loved by a parent, and I was therefore lovable. This man was white and would help me compensate for the shame, pain and inadequacies that I felt being black, and therefore I would be lovable. This man was large framed, physically strong and masculine. I felt that his masculinity made me feel complete because I was "light in my loafers," and therefore I would be lovable. I derived my sense of self worth through this man.

I had an excellent education, a wonderful job and a beautiful home that many could only dream about. I also had friends on the A list, wonderful pursuits and hobbies, so outwardly my life was fine. Inwardly my life was hell, but I was afraid to look at it because it was too scary, and I didn't have the tools. When the break-up occurred, I felt my life was over. It nearly drove me to suicide because I felt that my life force was leaving me when the relationship left. However, the break-up forced me to look at who I was, more clearly and more objectively. It forced me to look at the life force, as the source for all that I was.

I learned my sense of self worth could not come from another individual, a house, money or friends. It could not be dependent on any outward trapping because any outward trapping could be yanked away at any time. I learned that my sense of self worth must come from within me, based on my understanding that GOD loves me and that I love myself. By nurturing my relationship with GOD, my understanding of myself as an innocent and perfect being, and my new awareness of the universe, I found an inner peace that was independent of outward trappings. That inner peace came from a source that we all can tap – GOD.

This "big bang" caused tremendous pain and grief. I screamed, I cried, I raged, I wailed, and I thought that I would die. I asked GOD to heal my mind and heal my heart. To help me feel lovable, acceptable, and peaceful within myself – so that I never have to go through this life threatening situation again. I asked GOD to help me find the tools that I needed to heal myself and to feel this peace, fulfillment, and happiness. I asked GOD to help me escape the prison I had created for myself with my mind.

The tools I received are the tools that I share with you in this book.

Chapter Three

HOW WE BECAME IMPRISONED

Detour To A Place Called Thear

To understand how we have become imprisoned in erroneous beliefs and the pain that they have caused, we will take a detour to a mythical place called Thear. Thear is a place in the universe. Thear is a planet with living beings called Thearans, who evolved over time. In the beginning, these beings shared the planet with many other living beings. However, these other beings were bigger and stronger. The other beings had more natural defenses such as claws or fangs. As a result, these other beings preyed on the Thearans. The Thearans were vulnerable because they did not have shelter, a steady source of food, or similar defenses such as claws or fangs. However, the Thearans mastered their environment by mastering their minds. These Thearans also had something in great supply that many of the other beings on Thear didn't have as much of – spiritual energy. They had a stronger connection to a higher intelligence. The Thearans called it instinct, but this connection was really their connection to the universal source of life, and it helped them in many ways.

As the Thearans evolved, their struggles with their environment became less threatening, and they eventually mastered their environment. However, the perception that the world was a hostile place remained ingrained in their consciousness. As a result, the Thearans carried fear as an integral part of their psychological make-up.

To balance this fear, the Thearans also had a mystical fascination with that part of themselves that was connected to the infinite intelligence. They were enthralled by that part of their makeup that was SUPER, the part of them that could touch a higher power, the part of them that was above and beyond the physical body, and the part of them that was spiritual energy. These Thearans became so fascinated with the spiritual aspect of themselves, that they gathered together to study it. In many different times and many different places on Thear, these Thearans gathered together to study the nature of this spiritual energy, how it manifested in their lives and how it could be deliberately used to help improve their lives just as it had already been used.

So the Thearans continued to gather. However, they realized as they gathered more and more, and as the numbers of Thearans who were exploring this spirituality became larger, that they had to organize. As they grew they formed an organization in order to focus and organize their gatherings in a way that would maximize their efficiency. As a result, the organization that they formed became a living entity, or corporation unto itself (corp means "body" in latin). The objective of the organization (initially) was to foster the development and spiritual exploration of the Thearans.

However, over time, this primary objective became replaced by the "corporation's" objective of insuring its own survival because the organization had become an entity unto itself. This process was similar to the evolution of the March of Dimes' foundation. The March of Dimes was initially created to raise funds necessary to help polio victims. However, after polio was eradicated, instead of disbanding, the March of Dimes explored and supported the treatment of birth defects. This change in focus was to ensure the organization's survival.

In the case of the Thearans, they wanted to spread this organization and its influence throughout Thear. And they did. However, every few years the Thearans would conduct gatherings called Councils. The Councils were made up of leaders who had spread out over Thear to spread this philosophy. These councils, would get together and discuss common experiences that they had and common dilemmas that they faced in working with the Thearans and spreading this philosophy of spiritual exploration.

One of the common dilemmas that they faced was getting Thearans who were not like them to listen to what they had to say. These other Thearans had similar experiences to the Thearan "conquerers." However, these other Thearans had interpreted those experiences differently. So, during one of the council meetings the Thearans got together and said, "well these heathens and pagans aren't listening to us, because we believe in one supreme being and they believe in many supreme beings. We're having trouble relating to them because we believe in the infinite intelligence taking one finite form and they believe that the infinite intelligence takes many, many forms." So, during this rap session the Thearans decided to remedy the problem by creating a Trinity. In this Trinity, we can have three supreme beings instead of one. They said "Let's call one a father. Let's call one a son. Let's call one a spirit." This Trinity will help us to relate better to these pagans and heathens. The council members then went back and worked with these pagans and heathens with the concept of the Trinity and they were moderately successful.

Unfortunately for them, moderately successful did not give them the level of control that they desired. So they got together again in another council meeting and said, "These pagans and heathens still aren't listening to us. These pagans and heathens would still prefer their own individual experiences with divine intelligence to the experience with divine intelligence that we are trying to force on them. We don't like that because that limits the influence of our organization, and our organization must survive. So what are we going to do about this latest dilemma?" Then the council decided to tap into the primal fear that all Thearans had, based on their history. They had retained a consciousness of fear based on their collective memory of Thear as a difficult place to survive in. The Thearan "conquerers" said, "Let's tap on this fear. Let's call on our version of the infinite intelligence, the Supreme Being, who can harm, punish and destroy Thearans if they don't heed the word of our Supreme Being. Let's put the fear of GOD into the Thearans."

The Thearan "conquerors" then wrote a caricature of their supreme being that was an angry, punitive, destructive, and judgmental force. They felt that by using fear, the other Thearans would listen more closely to what the "Conquering" Thearans had to say. The "Conquering" Thearans were more successful with this approach and began to control most of the Thearans, in one way or another. As a result, the theology of the "Conquering" Thearans continued to grow, survive and prosper. However, individual Thearans continued to try to have their own experiences with this spirituality.

Let's call the exploration of spiritual essence the Thearans explored, Thearacism. Thearacism grew and prospered. And Thearacism's influence grew as it's power and control over the Thearans grew. However, there were always malcontents who wanted to stir up the stew. These "troublemakers" wanted to look closely at Thearacism and they deigned to disagree with Thearacism.

However, Thearacism had gained such power and such prominence that it could wield power over these individuals or groups who disagreed or questioned it. For about 2 hundred years, thousands of Thearans were killed because they deigned to disagree, or explore their own forms of spiritual experience. Disagreement with the dominant doctrine and personal exploration of spirituality was seen as witchcraft, heresy or treason.

The rules of Thearacism became more and more prominent and seemed to multiply from out of nowhere. These rules had a stamp of divine approval when they actually came from the mouths of fellow Thearans. One Thearan who barely escaped execution was a Thearan who dared to question Thearacism. This individual posted a list of 95 questions on a Thearan place of worship. An example of one question was: Why could a wealthy Thearan be shielded from the wrath of this apparently vengeful supreme being just by giving money. Of course this Thearan suspected that by giving money, Thearacism would prosper.

These are just a few examples of how Thearacism positioned itself firmly as the mediating entity between individuals and their spiritual expression. In doing this, Thearacism would continue to survive.

Thearacism did an excellent job marketing itself as the middle man between individuals and their own spiritual essence. It made Thearans believe that no Thearan could experience their own spirituality unless it went through Thearacism and its rules. Anything that was not Thearic dogma was seen as heresy.

Thearacism controlled the masses. Thearacism used fear, shame and guilt. These control tactics blocked Thearans from the individual experience of their spiritual nature (except through the mechanism of Thearacism). These manipulations removed Thearacism from the truth of spirituality. The fear, shame and guilt that Thearacism used became pervasive emotions that kept individual Thearans from realizing their spiritual nature. These emotions separated Thearans from their perfection, their beauty, their worthiness, and their connection with the supreme and Infinite Intelligence.

However, in time the fear, guilt and shame made Thearans realize there must be a better way. One-by-one they got their wake-up calls. Their internal alarm clocks said "I was not meant to live with fear and pain. I will not be denigrated, and unfulfilled. I want to be happy, complete, joyous, confident, loving and lovable." In essence I was meant to be a reflection of my true understanding of the Infinite Intelligence, which is all those things. Little by little Thearans realized that perhaps Thearacism has distorted this Infinite Intelligence, and blinded them to the truth. But through meditation and prayer, they could see again. Armed with this power, no one would ever make them doubt the truth again.

Thearans found a better way. One by one, Thearans realized that they no longer had to live in pain. Thearans began connecting with their own spiritual experiences. Thearans began re-connecting with the life-force that was within them. Thearans began understanding the energy that kept the electrons, protons and neutrons spinning, and that made everything on Thear, and they began connecting with that energy. They began to come to the realization that this energy was loving, peaceful and calming (unlike the caricature of that energy that was depicted by Thearacism in order to control them).

Individually the Thearans came into a New Age.

Chapter Four

THE DOMINANT CONSCIOUSNESS

The Prison of Our Minds

In the previous chapter, Thear was an anagram for Earth. Like Thearans, we have all moved to a rather unenviable place. How did we get to that place of emptiness, fear, doubt, frustration and anger? We know that we got there through a number of different experiences repeated throughout our lives. We know that place described in Chapter 1, which was my place of utmost pain, from which I emerged victorious. We all know this place. Perhaps we don't know it as well because we are unaware of those feelings or we simply block them.

The Dominant Consciousness,
Incubator Of The False Ego

We got there through our experiences. Now we are

beginning to dredge up some of those experiences. However, there was a backdrop that supported those experiences – the popular consciousness. The backdrop of the popular consciousness is like a petri dish that enables bacteria to multiply – it provides an environment that enables these experiences to occur. The popular consciousness supports the view that life must be seen through a veil of tears. The popular consciousness supports the view that life does not support an individual, that the Earth is a hostile place, that people are hostile, and that survival is difficult. It sponsors the view that nothing we can do can turn out right, and that there is always some force that will punish us and keep us in check.

We Believed the Hype

This view is perpetuated by our belief in it. This view is perpetuated by the media. Listen to the lyrics of a few love songs and you quickly see how we have become trapped: "I am nothing, nothing, nothing, if I don't have you." "Oh, baby love, why do you hurt me......?" "My world is empty without you baby." "Stop! in the name of love, before you break my heart." "I hate myself for loving you." "I who have nothing. I who have no one."

The media perpetuates these beliefs in other ways as well. Look at advertising. We are not good enough if we do not fit a certain category, use the "right" toothpaste, wear the latest fashions, drive the latest car, or smoke the sexiest cigarette, or drink the high-end of champagne and taste the good life. We believed the hype. However, the media is not totally the culprit. The media is simply a reflection of the dominant consciousness.

The Dominant Consciousness Helped
Form Our Individual Consciousness

Our subtle experiences have also formed our individual consciousness. For example, a child doesn't learn racism only from a racial epithet. That racial epithet confirms racism, but a child learns racism when a mother clutches that child to her more closely when a different type of person approaches. A parent passes this and many other poisons on to the child, based on that parent's experience. What gets passed on, from the media, from parents and from your experiences becomes your consciousness.

I observed a perfect example of a subtle incident that had a devastating effect on a person's consciousness when reading an interview of Janet Jackson in Newsweek magazine. Janet related a story of how an elementary teacher embarrassed her in front of the class, and the shame of the incident was held in her consciousness for years, and contributed to a two year bout she had with depression. In her own words "I never talked about it, so it stayed with me all those years. I felt not deserving, not good enough. Like, why do I deserve to have success? I'm not a smart person. You know what I mean: And the thing is, that's still the way I feel about myself sometimes."

You Exude Your Consciousness Like Cologne

Energy is never created nor destroyed, it simply changes form. Thoughts are a form of energy. Thoughts are energy waves that vibrate at a certain rate, just like sound and light are waves that vibrate at a certain frequency. Therefore, thoughts are THINGS, just like sound waves are THINGS. When you go to a rock concert, your ears ring and throb hours later even though the sound waves have dissipated. The energy of that sound continues to reverberate, and these reverberations affect you. Your consciousness is the amalgamation of your thoughts, and the vibrational energy of those thoughts continue to affect you in the same way. Your past experiences, your current situations and your potential future all have an energy, and you exude this energy like cologne. When you wear cologne, the invisible molecules of the cologne emanate from you, and others smell them through the nerve endings in their noses. You exude your consciousness in the same invisible, yet tangible way. Let's call this your energy field.

Your Energy Field Creates Your Experiences

The human energy field emits a vibratory wave (not unlike a soundwave, or a magnetic wave). This vibratory wave has a certain frequency, just like different musical notes are simply sound waves that vibrate at different frequencies. Our human energy field vibrates at a frequency that reflects the experiences of our past, our current situation and our probable future. As this frequency moves, it magnetically attracts people and events that are similar to it (like attracts like).

I experienced a perfect example of thoughts (and thus of predominating energy) magnetically attracting situations when I lived in the New York area. A good friend and I went out to buy things for breakfast. He constantly complained that New Yorkers were so rude – especially clerks, who were always particularly nasty. He told me that he often got into fights with clerks.

He complained about it so much I could almost see what was coming. We were in the checkout line with our fruits, and coffee, and the newspaper, and rolls — All the Sunday Morning essentials. My friend had placed the newspaper on top of a stand out of the clerks field of vision. After the clerk finished ringing up everything and asked for the money, my friend said, "You forgot the newspaper." The clerk of course had to void out the transaction and wasn't sure how to void it. As she fumbled about, my friend got increasingly angry and impatient, and demanded that the clerk ring up the newspaper separately. However, the clerk had already gone into the system and begun the voiding process, so she insisted on doing it "her way." Tension mounted, tempers rose, and as you might imagine, a real nasty altercation followed, complete with name-calling and the store manager's involvement. As we left, my friend said, "See, I told you these clerks are nasty. They're always getting into fights with me and you can't get good help." My friend didn't realize that he created that situation. By placing the newspaper out of the clerk's field of vision, he subconsciously created a situation that became a self fulfilling prophecy.

Your Thoughts Create Self-Fulfilling Prophecies

The concept of a self-fulfilling prophecy is very familiar to most of us. How many times have we heard that phrase? Most educators know that a child produces what you expect him or her to produce. If we continually tell a child that he is smart and capable, that child will perform to those standards. If we tell a child that he is dumb and lazy, that child will perform down to those expectations. This is another example of how one of our thoughts or beliefs can create our outer world. This concept is called: The Inner Cause and the Outer Effect. In the previous "supermarket story," my friend's belief was just a portion of his total consciousness, and this belief helped determine his experiences. The Inner Cause was the belief that clerks were nasty and confrontational, and the outer effect was that fight that was created.

If we look at our lives in total, and this law, the Inner Cause and the Outer Effect is just like any other law. It's like the law of gravity. We can't see the law of gravity, but if I drop a pen a million times, that pen will fall to the floor a million times. It's like the law of magnetism. We can't see the law of magnetism, but we know that it exists when we move a magnet along a pile of small metal shavings. We don't see gravity or magnetism, but they are scientifically proven laws. The law of Inner Cause and Outer Effect is just like those laws. We can't always see it happening, but we can certainly see the results. Take a minute and think about this, and then think about your consciousness — the things that you believe — think about how your beliefs have created your world, the job you're in, the situations on that job, the relationships you're in, and the situations with those relationships. Understand what you have created. Understand the beliefs that you hold that helped you to create your life. By taking a moment to understand how your thoughts, beliefs, consciousness and predominating energy have helped to create your world, you can begin to understand how the law of Inner Cause and Outer Effect has shaped your life.

Your Thoughts Reflect Your Deeper Beliefs

To believe means to accept something as being true or real — even if it isn't. Thoughts are the manifestations of our beliefs. We don't walk around everyday talking about what we believe. Our beliefs are ingrained in our minds. However, we do walk around every day thinking. We think about everything that we see. We think about everything that we touch. We think about everything, and the thoughts that we have reflect our beliefs. If you think you are unlovable, then you will think that the person you are attracted to could not possibly love you. You never really say, "you know I really believe that I'm unlovable," but your thought processes reflect that deeper belief. Your thought processes then become a part dominating energy, you exude this predominating energy and it attracts your experiences just like the perfume in a flower attracts a bee. Therefore you might find yourself being attracted to people who cannot be attracted to you in return. Your core belief (that you are unlovable) has created the experience of you being attracted to people who are unattracted to you.

To Change Our Experiences, We Must
   Change The Deeper Beliefs That Create Them

In lieu of the previous description, our consciousness (and the predominating energy that reflects our consciousness) creates our outer world. To find inner peace, we must transform the parts of our consciousness that no longer serve us and deny us peace. For example, as a black-gay-man, my consciousness was that the world not accept me, and would deny my desires. I once believed that the world would never understand me, would denigrate me, betray me and ultimately destroy me. However, that consciousness would not serve me well on the planet, so I have had to transform that part of my consciousness. My path was painful – but that pain woke me up. Had my life been a cake walk, perhaps I would not have been motivated to find a new truth. The pain made me realize that the predominating consciousness was not in truth, because it denied my peace, joy and abundance. So to transform our consciousness – we must first understand the false beliefs that got us into this mess in the first place. As our understanding increases and we learn to "own" our beliefs, we take the first step in accepting responsibility for our own life.

The Dominant Consciousness

To Transform Our Beliefs We Must Examine Them

Accepting responsibility may seem like a key buzzword for the new age, but it is much easier said than done. When you accept responsibility for your situations, you can no longer blame your past, your parents, your siblings, your children or your boss for any of your circumstances. However, you must also understand that accepting responsibility is NOT accepting blame for a situation. As you see the situation objectively, you will understand that the situation is neither good or bad – that is a judgment that you place on the situation – the situation just IS. The situation is simply a starting point from which you can assess your beliefs and begin to change them, and thus to change your life. Therefore, as you accept responsibility, you are not accepting blame. Instead, you are accepting POWER, for you begin accepting that you have the power to change your life by simply changing your beliefs.

On the next page, you will find a group of phrases. After stating each phrase, make a note of the first thoughts that come to your mind. DON'T EDIT your thoughts. Remember – you are the only one who will see this worksheet. Don't think about whether your responses are right or wrong, or whether you should or shouldn't hold the beliefs. Just finish the sentences with whatever pops into your mind. Remember — you are the only person who will read this, and you can be honest with yourself.

General Beliefs

❖ At work, I believe that...
❖ I believe that my partner...
❖ I believe that my body...
❖ I believe that sex...
❖ I believe that money...
❖ I believe that power...
❖ I believe that women...
❖ I believe that men.
❖ I believe that children...
❖ I believe that I...
❖ I believe that religion...
❖ I believe that spirituality...
❖ I believe that GOD...
❖ I believe that my parents...
❖ I believe that my friends...

Did you find that exercise to be interesting? Were there any beliefs that surprised you? We'll now examine some common limiting beliefs to begin to give you a new perspective.

The Dominant Consciousness

Common Limiting Beliefs

❖ *It Would Be Unfair...*

It would be unfair if I had what I wanted. The limitation of that belief is that it indicates that life is a zero-sum game — that if you win, someone else has to lose. In truth, life is not a zero-sum game. There are many instances in your life where when you win, someone else wins as well. Try to begin to think of the universe as infinite, with an ever-expanding array of possibilities. In an ever expanding universe, there is always infinitely more. Therefore having an advantage does not automatically place someone else at a disadvantage.

❖ *I can't because of who I am... (I'm a woman, older or a minority)*

❖ *I can't because of who I was... (poor, with a rough childhood, or I tried before and failed)*

These are learned beliefs that might be ingrained in our minds and limit us from realizing our potential. These may be beliefs that cause us to think that we can't do something, and therefore we manifest the failure. Remember, if we believe it, we create it. Therefore, if we believe the opposite of these things, if we believe in our power, if we believe in our ability, if we believe in our creative capabilities, then we can create what we desire. However, if we believe the opposite, then we can create the opposite. We can create beliefs and results that are affirming to us. We can create beliefs that give us joy instead of pain. We can create beliefs that give us fulfillment instead of frustration. We can create beliefs that give us peace, instead of anguish.

❖ *I don't deserve this...*

When we feel that we don't deserve something, we indicate that there is something bad about us or something wrong with us, and therefore we feel that we are unworthy. With this belief, we don't really embrace the truth about ourselves. The truth is that we are innocent and perfect beings. The truth is that we are lovable and capable, and that we are simply reflections of GOD's perfection. Feelings of being undeserving indicate that we are not accepting ourselves fully, and if we cannot accept ourselves, how can we expect the world to accept us?

❖ *My partner, parent or boss said I couldn't or won't let me...*

This belief gives others power over you. It also flies in the face of the fact that we can create our own reality! Remember that GOD is the ultimate source of our supply and our power. GOD uses people, places and situations as channels. If we look to GOD (instead of to our spouse, parent or boss) we create an infinite number of ways that our needs can be met. We can create our own abundance! We can create our own peace! We can create joy for ourselves! And we begin by examining and changing our beliefs.

On the next page, please list the beliefs that no longer serve you, AND a blueprint for better beliefs. In order to find those beliefs that no longer serve you, you might examine the belief exercise that you completed on the previous pages, and compare those beliefs with the examples of common limiting beliefs that were covered. You might also want to ask yourself if the beliefs that you listed (from the belief exercise) reflect unconditional love and the universe's unconditional support for you. Please complete this worksheet, and we will continue our journey.

Blueprint for Better Beliefs

— ❧ —

❖ *Beliefs that no longer serve me:*

❖ *Other things I want to eliminate from my life:*

❖ *Things I want to add to my life:*

❖ *Things I am thankful for in my life:*

Chapter Five

OUT OF PRISON

Opening to God

During the previous chapters, I have shared many personal experiences with you as examples of the old beliefs that did not serve me well. I had to change these old beliefs. By example, these old beliefs also gave you a sense of old beliefs that do not serve you well. You too will have to change those limiting beliefs. I also hinted at new, better beliefs that serve me well now, and that could serve you better than some of your old beliefs keeping you in pain. As you read on, you will find practical exercises and additional tools to help you develop more positive beliefs. You will also find additional examples from my own personal experiences of how I, and others, have practiced these new beliefs with much success.

If anything that I have shared with you thus far seems familiar, it is simply because my experiences are a reflection of the human experiences that we all share. Regardless of our race, gender, income, sexuality or any of the things that make us individuals, we have all had core experiences of denigration through which we have learned to see the world. Unfortunately, many of those experiences draw us further away from our spirituality. We often feel that we have lost that individual linkage between us and GOD. Somehow we feel unworthy because we do not perceive ourselves connected to GOD's Light. Therefore, others see us as vulnerable and control us through shame, manipulation and distortion. And no matter what we do we will feel that we're not good enough and we give others power over us.

Others compensate for this sense of inadequacy by feeling better about themselves at the expense of those who may (on some level) seem to be even more disconnected from the approval and Light of GOD. For example, those who are weaker, poorer, or those who have had even more denigrating experiences make easy targets. From day one, we learned to rank ourselves against other individuals. But there's always going to be someone who compares more favorably on one dimension or another. There will always be someone who is better than us at something, or younger, or smarter, or prettier, so we will always have this inner feeling of lack, and that inner cause will keep creating experiences of unworthiness in our outer worlds. So, as we begin to re-establish a connection with our spirituality, we begin to see ourselves differently. We begin to heal past perceptions, and thus we begin to heal our lives. With our new perceptions and beliefs, we create this new life, based on the New Truth that we are finding.

Into A New Understanding of GOD

Through the parable about the mythical land of "Thear," you probably have a better understanding of why you have been reluctant to expand your consciousness, tap into your inner power and move out of the realm of emotions that cause pain and suffering. Perhaps now you understand how powerful meditation can be when you use it.

Meditation is an important tool for our journey because it helps us to open our minds and clearly see the beliefs that we have formed. Meditation also gives us a calm, objective space from which to view the traumatic experiences in our past that have been created as a result of these beliefs. By viewing these events calmly and objectively, we can then clearly see old erroneous beliefs. Understanding those mistakes is the first step in healing them. By healing these flawed beliefs we no longer create situations for ourselves that reflect erroneous thinking.

After practicing meditation and visualization we find it much easier to work with the traumas in our lives. With meditation we can bring them up, examine them and heal the emotional scars that they have left on us. But there's a little more background that is useful for us to have, as we continue our Pathway to Inner Peace. It is important to know why meditation is so helpful.

Let's begin exploring why meditation is so important by asking "what do you feel when you meditate? Do you feel a force caressing you? A source of energy? A source of intelligence? Do you feel touched by a source of love that you perceive to be outside of yourself?" As you become more adept at meditation, you will feel this more and more. And you may begin to ask yourself, "What is this force? What is this source? Why does it offer me such sustenance, such peace, such affirmation and so many good feelings? Why does it give me such bliss, such comfort and such joy?"

This source is GOD! Meditation and prayer nurtures our direct connection with GOD, in our own way, in our own time and at our own choosing. This is what organized religions, perhaps, didn't want you to know. Organized religions do not want you to know this, because by knowing of your own direct connection with GOD, why would you need the organized religions, and therefore how could the organized religions survive? This is why many taboos were set in place. Many labels were put on those taboos; witchcraft, heresy, sin. The only sin is thinking that is not in alignment with the truth. The truth is that GOD loves us completely and unconditionally, that the universe supports us completely and unconditionally, and that we can love ourselves completely and unconditionally. The truth is that love is all that exists, and the fears (and the different forms that fear takes) blocks us from opening to this truth. The truth is that we never separated from GOD's love, we have only believed that we were separate, and created an illusion of separation based on this erroneous belief. The truth is that as we shift our beliefs, and as we transform ourselves through prayer and meditation, we can create new and better lives for ourselves.

Let's examine what happens in meditation once again. In meditation you experience feelings of bliss, feelings of joy, feelings of wholeness, feelings of completeness and feelings of affirmation. Is there anything remotely negative in this?

Absolutely not! What was given to you was truth. The truth of your lovability and perfection. You felt a side of yourself that felt you could accomplish unlimited things. You probably found your imagination unleashed more and more as a result. My experience of GOD energy has not been the experience of punishment, of a nasty, vengeful, punitive, hateful, petty GOD, that would keep us in pain and agony. My experience of the GOD energy has not been an experience of energy that would control us in any way. My experience of GOD, and the experience of GOD that many are having on earth today, is that of a loving GOD. Many are having the experience of a benevolent GOD. Many have come to understand an affirming GOD. And the experience of meditation where we experience GOD directly, sets us free from old beliefs that are not reflective of the truth of GOD's unconditional love.

Understanding the Escape Plan

With the blueprint that you developed in the previous chapter, you can begin to develop and support beliefs that are more affirming to you. You can now foster beliefs that will create for you what you desire, and learning to meditate has helped this process by enabling you to see the beliefs that you hold (and the difficult, painful situations that they have caused) more clearly. However, meditation also does something else. It opens the channel between you and GOD! What a provocative statement. Opening the channel between you and GOD!

What is the channel between you and GOD? It is the real information super-highway. We're not aware of this channel many times in our daily lives. We are not aware that GOD and the life force within us are connected, and that we strengthen this individual connection through prayer and meditation. You have probably heard the catch phrase "we are all one" before in your life. I think of us as grapes on a vine — we have many shapes, sizes and colors, and we come in different bunches, but the bunches are connected at the branches, and the branches are connected at the base. The base is connected at the root, and the root sprang from the seed. All the grapes came from the same root, seed and source, and all are connected to the source.

Building a Bridge to GOD

When we meditate, the energy that pours through our body comes from the source and gives us waves of bliss, comfort and peace. We feel more of the life force running through our bodies. We become more aware of the life force that already exists, and then we begin to build that life force within our bodies. What is that life force and what is this energy that starts flowing through us as we become more adept at meditating? Could this energy be part of a larger life force than the life force we perceive within us? Could this energy be a part of a larger force in total? Could this energy be part of GOD's energy? Could it be part of GOD's love? Could it be part of our spiritual essence flowing in us as we open to it? When we meditate, what we open is that channel between us and GOD. Initially it is a small cord, for many of our experiences and much of our conditioning have kept us unaware of our individual connection with GOD and our ability to connect and interact with the GOD-force. However, every time we meditate we open that channel more and more. Each time, we are strengthening our spiritual muscle in the same way that physical exercise strengthens our physical muscles.

So, let us call meditation listening to GOD. Many of the impressions that we get come not only from our internal senses, but also from that realm of the Infinite Intelligence – the realm of the higher life force. This is the life force that we perceive outside of ourselves. This is the life force that flows through everything. This is the life force that keeps the neutrons, electrons and protons that comprise all matter vibrating.

We've already established that this life force is like magnetism or gravity – we can't see magnetism, but we see evidence of it every time we see a magnet draw metal shavings to it, so we know it exists. We can't see or hear gravity, but we know that any object that we drop will fall to the ground, and we experience it keeping our feet planted firmly on the ground. We also know that dogs can hear frequencies that humans cannot. Therefore we know that energy exists outside the realm of our everyday human perceptions. So this life force is GOD's energy, spiritual energy, another energy that we can't see, or feel, except when we begin to experience it through meditation. Through riding this "information superhighway" we learn to talk to GOD and listen to GOD.

Prayer is Talking to GOD /
Meditation is Listening to GOD

So let's call meditation, Listening to GOD! And then let's call prayer, Talking to GOD! Between these two, one builds an information super-highway. Waves of energy are exchanged between our human energy field, and the Divine Infinite Intelligence. And just like exercising, anytime we exercise a muscle, it grows and gets bigger and stronger. Let's consider that information super-highway like an invisible muscle between our world and the world of infinite intelligence – the world of GOD's Unconditional Love. Every time we meditate and every time we pray, that connection gets greater and greater just like every time we lift weights our muscles get stronger and stronger.

As this connection continues to occur, we have a tangible, individual experience of GOD's Unconditional Love. As we experience GOD's Unconditional Love, we realize GOD has never withheld love from any of us. We have believed that individual connection with GOD was impossible, because the GOD-force was remote as we were flawed and unworthy. But as the truth of GOD's Unconditional Love becomes more clear, we realize our misconceptions have caused us pain, and that we have the power to change them.

Prayer and Meditation Build Our Bridge to GOD

As we continue our Pathway, we will use prayer and meditation to find the inner peace and power that will change our outer world. We will use prayer and meditation to take away the scars caused by painful experiences and fear, because these scars keep us from fully being who we are. Prayer and meditation will heal every aspect of our lives so we then can live our lives in the way that we were supposed to live — lives of joy, bliss, peace, comfort, and assurance, in connection with each other and with the Higher Power.

Chapter Six

MEDITATION

A Key Tool on the Journey

Meditation is simple, and as easy as breathing. Yet meditation requires discipline that you can and must learn. Meditation is simply quieting the mind and body, and shutting out the external senses. When you habitually shut out your external senses, your internal senses become a well-developed muscle. This awareness develops naturally due to the practice you gain through sensory deprivation. For example, blind people are deprived of the sense of sight, so a blind person has a more acute sense of hearing. Enhanced hearing has developed to compensate for the loss of sight. By the same token, an additional awareness develops naturally within you as you practice shutting out your external senses.

You may use these internal senses to unlock useful understandings, memories and information. That information will help you in understanding your motivations, your surroundings and your life. Meditation surrounds you with peace and comfort that you may not realize has been lacking in your life. You gain a sense of safety and security. In addition, there are the physiological benefits that you receive from the rest and relaxation that is a part of meditation. This rest and relaxation will aid in relieving your stress.

Meditation is a discipline, just like weight lifting is a discipline, however, mediation is much easier and less physically taxing. This discipline must be learned and comes with practice. Therefore, I've listed some tips on how to deepen your meditation below. These tips should speed your Pathway to Inner Peace.

Find the Right Space

To begin the discipline of meditation, it is important to have the right space. You should choose a space that is quiet and comfortable. You should choose a space that makes you feel safe and at home. A dear friend chooses her bathroom as the right space. She has several children and little privacy, so the only space that works for her is the bathroom – she can close the door, shut out the world and focus on herself!

Find the Right Time

It is also useful to choose the right time. I recommend meditating either the first thing in the morning or the last thing in the evening, because its then that you have the most control over your time. Clear your mind of all extraneous thoughts while meditating. One technique I use is to forcibly think back on the things that have happened in the prior 24 hours. Then, I force myself to think forward to the things I anticipate happening in the next 24 hours. I direct my mind to focusing on these things for a few minutes prior to going into deep meditation, proactively having these thoughts. Then I concentrate on preventing them from popping into my mind as distracting random thoughts.

Learn to Concentrate

After clearing my mind, I found that I still had trouble concentrating (it seemed that random thoughts were EVERYWHERE). I then started using the "candle" technique with much success. To use this technique, begin by concentrating on a candle and make a note of how long your attention stays on the candle before a random thought enters your mind. The more you concentrate on that candle, the longer the intervals become between the times that random thoughts enter into your mind. Think of it as timing labor contractions in reverse. Your ability to concentrate becomes better and stronger with practice.

Free Yourself of External Distractions

It is very important that the space be quiet. Remember, one of the objectives of meditation is to tune out the external senses so that you become more aware of the inner senses. So in addition to having a quiet, noise-free space, it should also be dark and free of visual distractions. You can do this by closing your eyes. You can also just darken the room. I started using a "blackout" mask (the mask airlines give you help you sleep on overseas flights). However, the pressure of the mask became more of a physical distraction, so I simply got up and turned out the lights. To further eliminate physical distractions, it is important that your meditation place be a comfortable space.

Overall, you must remember that there is no "right" or "wrong" way to meditate. Whatever works for you is fine.

Watch What Happens

As you become more attuned to your internal senses, you might find that your internal senses become more acute. You may feel things more clearly. You might find that your internal hearing becomes more acute. You hear that still, quiet voice inside, with your inner ear. You may get impressions more clearly. You might find that your imagination becomes more vivid. These expanded senses help you in gaining insights into yourself and others. You might find that you understand more than you understood before. For example in the prior chapter when we looked back at events that had shaped your consciousness in this life, these events were brought up. These events are brought up, not through your outer senses, but through your inner senses, as you become more in control of your inner senses. As you become more aware of these inner senses, you can use them to gain these insights, and these insights can give you the information that you need to heal your life, manifest all that you desire, and achieve inner peace. In other words, meditation is the Ferrari you'll drive in your Pathway to Inner Peace.

Strengthening Your Meditations

We will now do an exercise that is designed to guide you in ways that will develop your internal senses more fully:

✳ Meditation Exercise ✳

Place your hands in your lap, palms upward. And begin to concentrate on your breathing.

Breathe deeply.

Inhale deeply....and exhale deeply.
Inhale deeply....and exhale deeply.
Inhale deeply....and exhale deeply.

As you continue to inhale and exhale, notice that your breath has a rhythm.
✳
Focus on the rhythm of your breath.
✳
Understand that with the rhythm of your breath is your life force.

Continue to breathe and let your mind focus on your breath. When a random thought pops into your mind, move it back out of your mind. Mentally set it on a shelf and say, "I will deal with you later." And continue to breathe.

⁜

You have already thought about the things that have happened in the last twenty-four hours and the things that you anticipate happening in the coming twenty-four hours. As you realize that you have already moved these thoughts out of your mind, your mind becomes more clear and you continue to breathe.

⁜

As you continue to breathe, and as you notice the rhythm of your breath, you become calmer.

⁜

You become more relaxed.

⁜

You begin feeling this relaxation in the top of your head.

⁜

This relaxation falls down around your facial muscles.

⁜

And this relaxation falls down the back of your head, almost like warm oil... flowing over your body.

⁜

And it relaxes the muscles in the back of your neck.

⁜

And this relaxation continues to flow down your body like hot oil; relaxing your shoulders so that your shoulders begin to droop.

This relaxation continues to wash down relaxing your chest.... and moves down your arms into your hands.

Your arms and hands are relaxed.

This relaxation continues to dwell in the area of your chest and it relaxes your chest.

You feel a difference in your heart.

This relaxing energy continues to move down, and it moves down and into your torso.... touching all of the vital organs housed in your torso.

This energy continues to relax you.... and now moves into your buttocks and your sexual organs with love and acceptance.

This energy relaxes that area of your body. And you continue to relax.

This energy then moves down into your thighs and it moves down your calves, and it moves down into your feet, until it moves to the soles of your feet.

Your whole body is relaxed.....
All relaxed....
Relax...

You are now surrounded with the energy of relaxation. It feels like a warm, wonderful, comforting oil that surrounds your body and makes it relax. And with this relaxation you have an expanded perception. You have an expanded awareness. And you use that awareness in this meditation.

✣

In front of you, you see an orange.

✣

You examine this fruit, and in your mind's eye, you hold this orange in front of you.

✣

You examine it with your hand. You turn it over, you look at the navel, you look at the ridges in the skin, you look at the coloring.

✣

You hold it.

✣

You feel the weight of the orange. You feel it's texture. And then you feel your body's reaction to the orange.

✣

Are you salivating more in preparation of eating the orange? Do you feel the juices in your stomach flowing?

✣

To satisfy your hunger, you begin to peel the orange.

✣

First you stick your thumb in the navel and peel it.

✣

You now see yourself peeling it.

✣

Meditation
..81..

See yourself peeling it.

✳

Feel what it feels like to stick your thumb in the navel of the orange.

✳

Feel the juices squirting out of the orange.

✳

Feel the feeling as the peel tears back from the body of the orange.

✳

Feel the juice squirting.

✳

Now feel the juice running down your finger tips.

✳

Smell the aroma of the orange.

✳

Continue peeling the orange.

✳

Take the pieces of the orange peel and place them in a pile next to you.

✳

See the pieces of the orange peel in a pile.

✳

You have completely peeled the orange.

✳

See the remnants of the orange rind, around the actual body of the orange.

✳

Take the orange and separate it into it's parts.

Feel the juice from the orange beginning to dry on your finger tips.

✳

Continue smelling the orange.

✳

Now, instead of eating the orange, take the pieces of the orange and put them back. So that the orange is now whole.

✳

You see it just as you did before you separated it into parts. You see the remnants of the rind surrounding the orange.

✳

You see the peel of the orange in a pile next to you.

✳

Take the peel and play the videotape of you peeling the orange, in reverse.

✳

See yourself putting the peel back on the orange, in reverse.

✳

Visualize yourself putting the peel back on the orange, piece by piece...

✳

You are recovering the orange...

✳

Continue to see yourself recovering the orange until the orange is whole again.

✳

Feel the disappointment because you were unable to eat

the orange as you desired.

Feel the smoothness of the surface of the orange, now that the peel is back on the orange.

Hold the orange in it's wholeness again.

Continue holding the orange.

Continue working with it.

Thank the orange for participating in your journey back to your imagination.

Now bring your consciousness back to the here and now and we will continue working.

You are now situated again in the here and now.

You are fully present here.

Unleash Your Imagination

What we have done is one of many ways to unleash the imagination within all of us. Imagination gives us the opportunity and the power to begin to see things differently. Imagination gives us the power to begin to see the possibilities in our lives. With imagination, we can begin to see with a new pair of eyes – our "inner eyes." We can discern what is in truth, and what has been told to us that is not in truth. For what we have learned that is not in truth keeps us from living with joy, abundance and peace. Therefore unleashing and unlocking the imagination is the very *key* to our *Pathway to Inner Peace.*

Create Your "Concentration Scene"

At first, many people have difficulty with meditation. And I will explain and discuss some ways to begin to feel more comfortable with meditation. First of all concentration can be a challenge. One way to improve your concentration is to concentrate on an image that is already familiar to you. We will call this image your "concentration scene." Your concentration scene should be an image that is already firmly ingrained in your mind's eye. For example if you spend a great deal of time driving to and from work, your car windshield and dashboard are probably very familiar to you. Therefore you might focus on the dashboard of your car, because that is a picture that pops into your mind quite readily. Or you might place an imaginary writing tablet in front of you, and focus on a page of this tablet. If you spend a great deal of time staring at a computer, you might choose to focus on the computer's screen saver because that is a visual image that is firmly planted in your mind's eye.

You might begin by focusing on your "concentration scene" and see the number one pop onto the scene, then see the number two pop onto the scene, then see the number three pop onto the scene, then see the number four pop onto the scene. As you continue to count up, you also continue focusing on the screen. And you continue emblazoning that scene in your mind's eye. You could also choose to focus on a candle, and watch it flickering. You might also note how often random thoughts pop into your head and try to keep them at bay. Hopefully, you've already actively considered everything that happened in the previous 24 hours and everything that will or that you anticipate happening in the next 24 hours. This action should have already moved many of the random thoughts that could occur out of your mind. You already mentally put them on a shelf. And so your mind is more clear.

As you imagine your "concentration scene," note how often a random thought pops into your head. At first it might be relatively frequent, but as you become more practiced at it, the random thoughts pop into your head less frequently, and the interval between the random thoughts become longer and longer.

Mentally Construct Your Safe Space

Another thing you might want to do, is to spend some time mentally constructing your safe place. Mentally constructing your safe place can be a wonderful way to unleash the imagination and to unleash your creative energies. Your safe place can be mythical, it can be any place you want it to be. You can surround yourself with things or symbols of things that give you comfort and peace. It can be indoors or outdoors. It could be on a mountain. It could be in a river valley. It could be a wonderful palatial estate, in front of a wonderful babbling brook. You could be in an outdoor garden on the estate. And you can envision that you have all the tools that you feel you would need. You can create the tools that you would need for protection, such as an imaginary bubble, so that you'd know you are protected. You could create the tools for comfort, such as a comfortable bed, so that you'd know that you are comfortable. You could create the tools for safety, so that you know that you are safe. You might also create tools that you would need for your survival in your space, such as food, water, a printing press (to print money), a potters wheel to form other objects that you desire, and a movie screen that would help you see the scenes you might need to see. It is important to spend some time with your imagination constructing your safe place.

In addition to painting a picture of your safe place visually, you should also get acquainted with how you feel when you are in your safe space. How does the chair feel beneath you in your safe space? How does the wind feel, as it gently, caresses you in your safe place? What sounds if any do you hear when you are in your safe space? Construct this vision of your safe space and work with it. Stay with it so that if at any time you need to return to your safe space in your mind, the vision is clear. The following page contains a worksheet to help you focus on your safe space. It also includes some suggested tools to place in your space. You can use it to help you construct your space.

Meditation
. . 87 . .

Your Safe Space is the Launching Pad for Your Journey

Your safe space is the launching pad

For moving back to peace
For moving back to comfort
For moving back to joy
For moving back to abundance
For moving back to all that we feel that we have
lost in this life.

The next page gives you an opportunity to describe and develop this "safe space."

My Safe Space

....Physical Description of My Safe Space

It is located...

It is surrounded by...

It has...

Tools I have in my safe space...

When I am in my safe space I feel...

Chapter Seven

THE SIMPLE TRUTH

New Rules for the Road

Prayer and meditation can help us find the "truth" of GOD – not what someone tells us about what GOD is, and says and wants, but because we experience GOD for ourselves. The truth can actually be quite simple. GOD loves us, completely and unconditionally. Regardless of our gender, regardless of our age, regardless of our race, regardless of our socio-economic background, regardless of our family circumstances, regardless of how we feel about ourselves. *GOD's love for us is complete and unconditional.*

The second truth is just as simple. *The universe supports us completely and unconditionally.* The universe is a place where we draw our support and sustenance. The universe is also a place that is reflective and indicative of GOD's love. GOD's love is simply the life force, the energy that flows through all matter in the universe, that which is animate and that which appears to be inanimate. The third truth is that *we can love ourselves completely and uncondi-*

tionally. And so we ask, *"If these are the truths then why am I not living in that truth now?"* The third truth becomes more central then. We do not experience unconditional love, because there are places where we do not love ourselves unconditionally. The universe is simply a reflection of our individual consciousness, and reflects that lack of love we feel for ourselves. We have been manipulated by organized religions to create a reality that is not in alignment with the truth. We've been manipulated by the media, and by our society to also feel less than whole based on our gender, race, sexuality or our past. We've seen what this conditioning creates in our society — racial strife, sexual tension, self hatred and division.

We often reject ourselves and deny ourselves pleasure and joy. We've been conditioned to the point where we believe that life should be seen through a veil of tears. We believe that life should be a painful struggle. We have believed that life should be anything but what it is meant to be – Bliss! We have forgotten how to feel good. We have forgotten that state of bliss and that we experience when we go into prayer and meditation. We feel disconnected from that state of oneness, that state of being with GOD. We feel disconnected from that part of us that is Divine. As a result, it is odd for us to feel that divine energy coursing through our bodies. But, our task as we choose to accept it, is to make this new "odd" feeling the natural state of affairs. This is the way it should be. We will create an existence where we will forget to hate ourselves. We will create so much inner peace, that we will forget to create painful situations for ourselves. We will no longer deny ourselves any of the joys and plea-

sures that are our divine birth rights. We will forget everything except who we truly are – *beloved children of GOD
who are innocent and perfect.* We are beloved children of
GOD who are manifestations of GOD's light. We will create
new, exciting possibilities. And we will enjoy the fruits of
those possibilities, which is bliss.

Navigating in the Garden of GOD's Love
 (Who or What is GOD?)

GOD (also known as the Infinite Intelligence, or the
ONE, or the Creator, or the Higher Power, or All That Is) is
simply energy. This energy is simply and purely Love. This
energy is evident in everything. It is the energy that holds
neutrons, protons, and electrons together. It is the energy
that forms our creation. And it is the energy that pours
through every living thing. This Is GOD! This has been my
experience of GOD.

Many times we need to put a finite name and face on
GOD due to our limited consciousness. Our perceptions
have been limited primarily to what we can see, hear, and
feel. At one point in evolution, this limitation was necessary
because the limited consciousness enabled us to focus solely
on survival. Unfortunately, by focusing so much on the here
and now, humanity learned to block out information from
the other realm. So we discount the simultaneous existence
of the human and the spiritual realm. As a result, we only
understand GOD through a filter of our limited consciousness. Therefore we have to put a name, a face and character-

istics on this energy which actually has no name and face because it is infinite. We've also accepted many distortions of this energy. In prior chapters we've looked at how many of these distortions formed. In summary we've accepted distortions that this GOD energy was vengeful, punitive, and would exact a high price on us and on our souls due to our pursuit of joy. We now understand that the caricature of GOD I just described was painted by organizations who simply wanted to control the masses to ensure their own survival, and insert themselves firmly between the individual and GOD to block the individual from experiencing their own individual spirituality.

We now understand that their objective in doing this was to maintain their own power and maintain the survival of the organization. So, through prayer and meditation we re-establish an individual link with GOD. As a result, we begin to have a different experience of GOD.

We begin to have an experience of GOD as an all enveloping and loving energy. We begin to have an experience of GOD as consciousness, and we begin to understand that this consciousness loves us completely and unconditionally. We begin to understand that this consciousness pervades all things. We are all individual expressions of this consciousness, in the same way that a beautiful painting is an expression of the consciousness of the painter. GOD had this wonderful mosaic called earth, and this wonderful mosaic called the physical universe, which has been created out of the consciousness of unconditional love. We are all a part of that consciousness, simply individualized specks on the painting of GOD's consciousness. We are individual expressions of GOD's consciousness.

The Simple Truth

This truth is very interesting because it says that as an individual expression of GOD's consciousness, we carry the same characteristics that GOD has – *Infinite power, infinite wisdom, infinite love,* and the capacity for *infinite joy.* However, the same circumstances that have caused us to feel like we were unable to touch the hem of the robe of GOD, so to speak, helps us to believe that we are separate from GOD. In truth, we are an integral part of the beautiful picture of GOD's creation. We also feel that we are separate from GOD because as expressions of GOD's creation, we have created situations that seem unlike the unconditional love of GOD.

What we must understand about what we have created is that we have done so out of our free will. If you now understand that GOD is not vengeful or punitive, you must also understand that the energy of GOD would not control us in any way, because that would restrict the creative power that was unleashed as a result of our creation. Any restriction of this creative power would be at odds with the reason for our creation, which is to simply experiment and expand the creative energy of the universe. Therefore, we have free will with which to create our experiences.

Although some of the experiences that we have created have caused us and others pain and suffering, they have also been a catalyst for us to "wake up" and explore a new truth. Now that we can create with this new truth, we can appreciate even further the Bliss of GOD, for we have a deep understanding of the pain created when we are not in alignment with the energy of GOD.

Of course, many of the things that we have created with this free will have not been aligned with GOD's love. They have been reflections of a different consciousness and we feel guilty about what we have created. We also feel guilty because as individual expressions of GOD's love, we feel that because we emanated from the light of creation, that somehow we have left the fold. We need to understand that we have never left the fold, we have simply expanded it, and we will always be part of the fold. We have never left the Garden of GOD's Love, we are the flowers of his Garden.

Re-Aligning With The New Truths

The consciousness of separation that was just dispelled was not in alignment with GOD's truth. Therefore, it gave us an opportunity to align ourselves more fully with the truth, and therefore, to align ourselves more fully with affirming situations. All of our consciousness creates the situations that show us where we are aligned with GOD's truth. We also create the situations that show us where we are not aligned with GOD's truth. Situations which are painful or difficult cause our souls to cry out. Situations such as the "Big Bangs" described before cause us to question our very existence and the love of GOD. Situations where we feel unfulfilled, unloved and unhappy show us where our consciousness is not aligned with the consciousness of GOD. On the other hand, where we feel fulfilled, happy and loved, shows us where we are aligned with GOD's truth; which is simply unconditional love.

We have created these situations as benchmarks to gauge where we are in alignment with the truth of GOD, and where we are not. These situations are also sign-posts, for they clearly show us our misperceptions, so that we may heal them. As a result, we create a RE-union/RE-alignment. Incidentally, re-alignment is the source of the word religion, which means to re-lign or to be back in alignment with GOD. We create this re-alignment with GOD by heeding the guideposts of our lives. This is achieved by looking at our lives and our situations, and seeing where they are affirming, joyful, loving, fulfilling and peaceful, and seeing where they are not. Where they are not, we understand that we are going in the wrong direction. Where they are, we understand that we are going in the right direction. And a good barometer is examining our beliefs, as we have done in the belief exercise. Examining what these beliefs have created in our lives, and then assessing whether that is aligned or unaligned with three basic premises. If we keep these premises very simple, everything else falls out of these premises. The three truths that we can bounce our perceptions and beliefs off of are:

1.. GOD loves us completely and unconditionally.

2.. The universe supports us completely and unconditionally.

3.. We can love ourselves completely and unconditionally.

Now let's look at some examples of how these all work.

Much of what has been ingrained in our minds is that GOD hates us because "he" is a hateful, vengeful GOD who exacts a huge toll on us if we choose to experience anything that "he" does not want us to experience. Much of this misinformation has been due to translation errors that distorted the essential truth contained within the Bible. According to Dr. Rocco Errico, there are thousands of translation differences in the Bible. Dr. Errico is a noted biblical scholar who helped translate the Bible back to its original Aramaic language. He placed the words of the Bible in the context of the time when it was written. He found that the "figures of speech" used are now taken literally (in the same way that we say "I've been chained to my desk all day"). Imagine how that will sound in 2,000 years. Can you envision a ritual and a holiday called "Chain Day" where people chain themselves to their desks to bring about business success? He also noted the customs of the times including the penchant for exaggeration, which made events more memorable in the absence of many written records. He also noted the mistranslations due to language differences because the Bible has been repeatedly translated into various languages over hundreds of years. When we consider these facts, it is not surprising that there are so many misperceptions of the Bible. When you add that the interpretations of many of the Bible's original intent may have been twisted by the few to control the many, it is no wonder that the Bible seems to be used more like a weapon of hate than like a tool of Love. Bruce Bawer offers a very lucid explanation of how this occurred in his recent book entitled: "Stealing Jesus." A perfect (and simple) example of how the truth has been twisted can be found in the phrase "GOD is a jealous GOD." The original translation of this text was GOD is a ZEALOUS GOD, meaning a very active and present force, which has a totally different meaning, and does not paint GOD as an angry caricature!

In truth, GOD wants us to experience all. As individual expressions of GOD, we were created to experience all that we could, in order to continue to expand the canvas of creativity that is GOD. Because we have felt that GOD does not love us, we have also felt undeserving of many good situations in our lives. On a deeply subconscious level, we may feel that we don't deserve that better job, and therefore we create situations that keep us in a job that is unsatisfying. On a deeply subconscious level, we may feel that we are undeserving of a joyful and fulfilling relationship, so we find ourselves continually creating relationships that are not fulfilling for us. We may feel that we are undeserving of happiness and peace, so we find ourselves creating situations which offer us a countless variety of ways to experience turmoil. We are painting the canvas with our consciousness, but we are painting a canvas based on the consciousness that we possess. Our task is to begin painting with a NEW brush, based on the truth that GOD loves us completely and unconditionally.

Much of what we created was out of fear of punishment, and we see the results of what we create. Therefore, we must know that the Universe supports us completely and unconditionally. We find that when we are not aligned with this truth, the universe does not seem to support us. Things do not seem to fall into place effortlessly. Our lives seem to be difficult and "traffic" in every aspect of our lives always seems to be snarled. Think of the frustration of sitting in snarled traffic, and think of how that frustration might permeate every aspect of our lives when we believe that the Universe does not support us completely and unconditionally.

I have a very interesting observation of how my consciousness changed my experience with this change. The Inner cause was, that the universe didn't support me. The Outer Effect was that everything always seemed to get gummed up. Communications between others seemed to get gummed up, even to the point where it seemed like the mail in my life couldn't be delivered on time. However, things changed as I became more aligned with the truth of the universe's complete support for me. I manifested jobs that steadily decreased my commuting time from two hours, to 30 minutes, to 15 minutes. My current commuting time is the time that it takes to get from my bedroom to my HOME office. No more traffic! That's a simple analogy, but if you look at the traffic patterns in your life, everything in your life that you want to get done and the hassles and frustrations of your life, you may realize that this has been created due to a belief that the universe doesn't support you. You may still believe that you're always going to get into the check-out line that has the slowest check-out person, and they will always change the money tray as you approach. You may subconsciously believe that you're always going to be stuck behind a slow-moving truck or school bus on your way to work. You may still believe that you're never going to get the job or the fulfilling relationship that you want. These experiences are created out of your belief that the universe does not support you. However, when you change that belief, the circumstances of your life become much easier to navigate.

If the previous two truths are easy for you to accept, then it should be just as easy to give yourself permission to have complete and unconditional loving acceptance for yourself. Unfortunately, most of what we have created thus far in our lives has been created out of the opposite of this truth, which is self-rejection. Many times we find it difficult to completely love and accept ourselves. The mass consciousness tells us that if we don't have small noses and Aryan features that we aren't lovable and acceptable. The mass consciousness tells those who have small noses and Aryan features that they don't deserve what they have gotten because it is based on their looks. What a dilemma! The mass consciousness tells us that if we weren't born with a silver spoon in our mouths and don't have the right family that we are nothing. If our families didn't come over on the Mayflower, or if we didn't fit some social ideal or standard we were nothing. But, that same consciousness told those who had this exalted social standing you were still nothing, because you didn't earn it.

A study was done of wealthy people. Some had inherited wealth. Some had made wealth. Some had won wealth. What they found was that they all had a feeling that they deserved their wealth. They had little else in common, but they believed that they deserved their wealth and this belief opened them to create (or maintain) their wealth. The mass consciousness gives us many, many reasons to not accept ourselves completely and unconditionally, and thus to feel that we are undeserving. We do not fit those lofty standards that no one truly fits. Perhaps we are not of the "right" gender.

Perhaps we are not the "right" age. Perhaps we are not of the "right" ethnic group. Perhaps we are not of the "right" sexual orientation. Perhaps we are not of the "right" socio-economic group. This brief list is just the tip of the iceberg, for there are a "myriad" of "conditions" that we place on our ability to love and accept ourselves completely. Our human identity has many dimensions. I can't think of anyone who would rank highest on all dimensions, so we've all placed these "conditions" on our ability to love ourselves. Our experiences have confirmed these "conditions," and as a result, we sometimes have difficulty learning to love ourselves completely and unconditionally.

We must remember that on the level of our soul, which is a part of the infinite intelligence, we chose the situations that we find ourselves in. We chose the parents, the socio-economic group, the racial identity, the gender and the sexual identity. We chose these experiences so that they might give us the "wake-up calls" that we need to re-align us with the unconditional love of GOD.

To understand this concept more fullly, let's visualize the following scenario:

Imagine the "source" or the center of the Universe wanting to expand and create new experiences. In order to do so, the source erupts like a volcano (with a big bang) and creates individualized particles of its essence. These individualized particles then expand outward from the source to the "edges of the universe" in order to expand the "source's" range of experiences and creations. These individualized particles are infused with the same qualities of the source – unlimited creative power and unconditional love, which is the essence of the source. These individualized particles have been charged to go out and explore, experience and create. When they are finished exploring, experiencing and creating, they will then return home to the core of the "source," augmenting the experience of the "source." While they are exploring, however, they will always be connected to the source because they have never left the "source," they have simply expanded the "source."

However, as these individualized particles move further and further away from the source, they began to misperceive that they had in fact left the "source." They began to see themselves as separate from the "source" and separate from each other. They began to judge themselves and others because some seemed to be closer to the source and others seemed to be further from the heat and light of the source. They began to see others as "better" or "worse" than themselves based on their relative position to the "source." This separation began causing conflict between groups.

These individualized expressions also misperceived that they had somehow left the fold, and they began feeling the guilt of an errant child. They forgot that in truth they had simply expanded the light of the "source." They forgot that they were truly a part of the source. This guilt compounded, and they began to misperceive the "source" as a stern parent from whom they had strayed. They began to misperceive the "source" as judgemental, angry and vengeful. They then used their unlimited power to create scenarios or dramas based on these misperceptions.

In truth, parts of these "individualized expressions" of

the "source" had forgotten their true power, beauty and perfection. Parts of their consciousness had become steeped in anger (because they misperceived that they had been abandoned by the "source") and guilt (because they misperceived that they were flawed because they had strayed from the "source"). These misperceptions were false, and made the "individualized expressions" vulnerable to pain and suffering.

As a result, the Earth (also known as the theatre in the round) became a place where the misperceptions of the individualized expressions could be "played out." As you have guessed, these "individualized expressions" are the individual souls that are a part of you and me. Although the vast majority our souls (our higher selves) are resident in the realm of the "source," a part of our soul's expression has been made manifest on earth so "play out" these dramas, realize the misperceptions, and heal these misperceptions so that all the soul's consciousness can return to the "source," as all the soul's consciousness is once again vibrating in the unconditional love that is consistent with the energy of the "source."

In the meantime, here we are, in the "theatre in the round" called Earth. Think of this Earth drama as a "B Grade" monster movie from the fifities. In this drama, the pretty woman (I apologize, but the victim always seemed to be a pretty woman) was approaching a door. In the audience, you knew that there was a monster behind the door, but the victim didn't. As you saw her approaching the door and heard her footsteps clicking, you would scream "don't open the door!" Of course the victim always opened the door. Well your soul energy is sitting in the audience in the "theatre in the round" called Earth, guiding you as much as possible, screaming "don't open the door" when we repeat patterns and perpetuate thought processes that cause us pain and suffering. We open to this soul energy in times of crisis as we cry out for divine help, and as we request this help and open to receive this help, it comes flooding to us.

As a part of this process, your human self is able to merge with more of your soul's energy (the part of you that is unlimited and powerful) and you become enlightened. You open to this enlightenment because you give the divine source permission to work within your mind, your body and your affairs, in order to bring peace and comfort to you in times of distress. In your distress signals, you give the universe and the "source" permission to heal you.

You may ask: "if the "source" is omnipotent and omnipresent, why do I have to give permission?" You have to give permission because part of your original charter was that you would create with your free will, and nothing could override that free will.

You may also ask: "why does this path seem to invariably involve pain and suffering?" The pain and suffering that we have experienced as humans is the catalyst for the growth and re-alignment that we desire on the level of our souls. In the eternity of the soul, and from the perspective of the soul, the pain and suffering is only a temporary illusion, just like the illusion on a movie screen that you make real with your mind.

Your soul chose difficult circumstances in order to grow, know its true identity and re-align with the true nature of GOD. From the point of the infinite intelligence where the soul truly resides, the momentary pain and discomfort that these "wake-up calls" cause are simply brief episodes, because the soul has an infinite life span. The soul sees this Earth drama as a stage play, an illusion. The soul is like an objective observer that knows that the pain and discomfort is just a small portion of its total experience (most of which is blissful). The soul says: "I can deal with this experience because in the infinity of my experiences, this is just a blip on a radar screen." The soul says: "I'll choose this situation that will give me some unaffirming experiences. These unaffirming experiences will cause me pain, and this pain will compel me to choose another consciousness. This pain will cause me to experience what the lack of love can create, and this will force me to love myself completely and unconditionally, because I will no longer want to create pain and suffering for myself."

The soul creates this drama and plays many parts. Through trying on many masks, the soul comes into a deep realization of the truth of its identity. The soul discovers that it is neither black, nor white, nor straight, nor gay, nor young, nor old, nor male or female, nor rich, nor poor, nor healthy, nor sickly, nor wise, nor stupid – *it is all those things* – for it has been all those things at one point in this long drama called humanity. In truth, the soul is none of those things, for it is simply a creation and reflection of GOD. It has chosen these many experiences because they cause you to place "conditions" on your ability to love and accept yourself completely. By moving through what these "conditions" create, you learn love and accept yourself more. By moving through what these "conditions" create, you will no longer believe anything but the truth of GOD's unconditional loving acceptance for you. Therefore, you will have a deeper experience of GOD's unconditional loving acceptance. By experiencing what a lack of unconditional loving acceptance can create, you will not create it anymore. You will simply learn that you are loved completely and unconditionally and you will reflect only that love. As a result, ALL of your soul essence will vibrate only with complete and unconditional loving acceptance, and you will evolve your soul. As you vibrate with unconditional loving acceptance, you are more aligned with the energy of GOD, which is complete, unconditional loving acceptance.

As the soul evolves into this complete alignment with GOD, the soul moves closer and closer to the source of all, and goes back "home" to the center of creation from whence it came. However, it goes back home with a litany of experiences, and with a legacy of its creations that enhances the overall creativity and experience of GOD, and in doing so, fulfills its task as an individual expression of GOD.

The light of GOD's love has flooded the Earth, and this flood brings an opportunity for Grace. The law of Grace is the transformational law that enables us to immediately stop creating painful situations, for the Amazing Grace of GOD transforms our minds so that we are no longer lacking in love for ourselves. Through GOD's Grace, we can begin creating new, wonderful experiences through the work we are doing in our Pathway to Inner Peace.

Therefore, we can continue our Pathway by using the phrase "I love myself completely and unconditionally" as the third premise of the simple truth. We can examine our lives to see what we have created with this simple truth. We can ask ourselves: "Have we created a situation where we have a lover who can or cannot love us completely and uncondi-tionally? Have we created parents or children who can or cannot love us completely and unconditionally? Have we created situations in our lives that do or do not affirm us completely and unconditionally, instead of affirming us based on our name, rank, and serial number? So, in summary, the new truth is quite simple. The new truth is this: GOD loves us completely and unconditionally. The Universe supports us completely and unconditionally. We can love ourselves completely and unconditionally.

1.. *GOD Loves Me Completely and Unconditionally.*

2.. *The Universe Supports Me Completely and Unconditionally.*

3.. *I Can Love Myself Completely and Unconditionally.*

The New Truth

As we shift our consciousness to reflect only this new truth, our consciousness can only create situations that reflect this new truth. Anything else that is created, is created simply to show us where we are not in alignment with this truth, and we now will have the tools to transform this consciousness. With these tools, we can create a new experience of life on Earth for ourselves.

There are three keys to clearing this consciousness.

Affirmations, Prayer and Meditation, and Emotional release. And we will talk about the role of each of these in the next chapter.

Chapter Eight

TRAVELING TOOLS

Living Your New Truth

Affirmations

Affirmations are universal truths, or statements of fact that you would like to be your truth. To truly understand the power of affirmations, let's explore the power of a lie again. If you tell a lie ten times, by the tenth time you tell the lie, that lie has become the truth. Of course the first time you tell the lie, it's a lie. The second time you tell a lie, it's still a lie. The third time you tell a lie, you've embellished it just a bit. The fourth time you tell a lie, you've embellished it just a little more. By the fifth time you tell a lie, you have probably created a story around it, so now you are telling a story. The sixth time you tell a lie, that story becomes stronger and stronger. The seventh time you tell a lie, that story becomes cast in concrete. By the tenth time you tell a lie, it has become so deeply embedded in your mind as a story that it has become the truth. Your perception has shifted, and you actually believe the story on some level. Because you have told that story so much through your words, because you have thought about that story so much in your mind, that story has actually become the truth.

You can have a similar experience by using affirmations. Affirmations are universal truths (or truths that we would like to experience). When you keep telling yourself these truths, they seep into your mind, your energy field, and eventually into every cell of your being in the same way that the dominant consciousness has seeped into your energy field. As a result, you then experience only the truth that has become part of your predominant energy. By understanding the power of a lie to change what you believe, you can also understand the power of affirmations. Affirmations can change your beliefs and align them with the Simple Truths. Examples of some affirmations follow:

General Affirmations of Love to
Raise Your Vibration

———

    ☙ *I am a beloved child of GOD.*

    ☙ *I love myself completely and unconditionally.*

    ☙ *GOD loves me completely and unconditionally.*

    ☙ *The Universe supports me completely
       and unconditionally.*

⚘ I am the light of GOD in manifestation.

⚘ I am innocent.

⚘ I am perfect.

General Affirmations of Unlimited Openness

⚘ What is GOD s belongs to everyone.

⚘ What is GOD s belongs to me and is my due.

⚘ I am open to receive.

⚘ I have an unlimited capacity to receive.

⚘ GOD is the source of my supply and my unlimited abundance.

⚘ I accept prosperity as my divine birthright and I do so without guilt because I love myself completely and unconditionally.

Affirmations of Creation

⚘ Everything I see begins and ends with me. My consciousness creates it. Therefore I will create only loving and affirming experiences for myself.

❧ The creative power of GOD manifests through me in a clear and undistorted way.

❧ I have an unlimited capacity to create my desires.

Affirmations of Your True Identity

❧ I am innocent and I am perfect.

❧ GOD is the source of my supply and my unlimited abundance.

❧ I am beautiful. I am lovable. I am adequate.

❧ In the infinity where I am, I accept myself as perfect, whole and complete.

❧ There is a divine plan for my life and that plan is unfolding for me now.

❧ I accept my place as a beloved child of GOD.

Affirmations for your Body

❧ My body responds in a perfect way to physical exercise.

  ✌ My body is a temple of light, and serves me perfectly to teach me to love myself completely and unconditionally. Where I am not loving my body, it teaches me where I do not love myself, and as I love my body more completely and unconditionally, I take only actions that glorify it.

Affirmations of Transformation

  ✌ There is a divine intelligence and that divine intelligence is working through me now.

  ✌ I alone can't do it, but The Christ Within me can and is creating miracles in my mind, body and affairs, here and now.

  ✌ The Light of GOD transforms my mind, my body and my affairs.

  ✌ Positive thoughts create all the advantages and benefits I desire.

General Affirmations

  ✌ I surrender to GOD s will for me. GOD s will for me is to have all the things that I desire. GOD s will for me is to have all the experiences that I desire. GOD s will for me is to have all the joy that I desire.

 ✍ *As 1 open to my innocence and perfection, 1 release my guilt and pain.*

 ✍ *1 love myself for being me.*

Of course there are as many affirmations as there are states of existence that we wish to experience. This is a small sample of affirmations that can help us with our lives.

When we affirm, we implant new truths in our minds and (to some degree) into our energy fields, and thus we begin to create with these new truths. However, affirmations alone are not enough. For example, if the mind creates based on one truth, yet the energy field holds memories based on "old truths" that we have experienced in the past, then there is an inherent conflict and the mind has difficulty creating. It's almost like building a house on a foundation of quicksand; you can build the house and the construction can be solid, but if the foundation is quicksand then the house will not be supported. Therefore, it is important to supplement affirmations with the emotional clearing that will clear the rest of the energy field.

Emotional Clearing

Emotional Clearing enables the rest of the energy field to catch up with what the affirmations have created in the same way that the foundation supports the construction of a house. Unfortunately, emotional release is something that is not well understood and not well used. It has been avoided because we have been conditioned not to have our emotions. In order for us to have an orderly society we were socialized to subjugate emotions in deference to a greater harmony. A cycle of subjugation occurs because as we suppress more and more emotion, we become even more afraid of the sheer range, depth and power of the suppressed emotions.

Imagine the range of events that humans have experienced on the planet over eons of time. Because the earth has seemed like an awful place for much of this time, most of these experiences have generated pain, suffering, lack and terror.

Now imagine that much of these emotions have been bottled up, and are contained in the soul's energy. The soul, then, recreates experiences based on this recurring energy pattern and the pain and suffering seem to multiply. The pain and suffering multiply until they explode like an over-taxed pressure cooker. These "opportunities for release" are the "big bangs" that I referred to earlier. These are the wake-up calls that change our lives.

In 10 words or less, our emotional state (our energy field) can make us sick. The contracted, conflicted energies block that spiritual energy (or light) that keeps our minds, bodies and affairs in alignment. This misalignment can cause us harm. The misalignment occurs because the constricted, contracted energy of anger and pain is suppressed and cannot move. Misalignment blocks our energy field from attracting and retaining the spiritual energy (or light) that would keep it in balance and attract positive experiences, because this spiritual energy is not consistent with the contracting energy of anger and pain (remember, like attracts like). Instead, due to the law of inner cause and outer effect, negative experiences are magnetically drawn to us because that is what we are holding in our energy fields. Imagine a water hose that has a "kink" in it, or your car's fuel tank when there is debris in it. In both cases, what is needed for proper functioning cannot be dispersed. The water in the hose cannot nurture the flowers in your garden (so they wither), and the gasoline in the tank cannot move through the fuel line to power your car, so it cannot function efficiently (if at all). In that same way, the light of GOD which nourishes us cannot provide its full benefit to us due to blockages in our energy fields.

Imagine yourself as a human vacuum cleaner, drawing your reflection to you – if your dirtbag is full, you cannot draw anything else to you. Therefore, there is a need to clean out your emotional dirtbag so that you can vacuum in new, good things.

There are many examples of the manifestation of this law of "inner cause" and "outer effect." Some examples of the emotional state affecting the body include butterflies in the stomach, also known as stage fright. Stage fright is simply energy within the solar plexus (the emotional center) that needs to move out due to anxiety or fear. That's the mind telling the body, "I feel fear. I feel anxiety. I need to move this fear and anxiety out of my energy field (and out of my body)" so we have butterflies in the stomach to make us aware that something is amiss. We've all heard legends about famous performers who get physically ill before a performance. Usually the imbalance fades when the performance begins because through performing, they move the energy of fear out of their energy fields (it fuels their performance).

I was reminded of the law of "inner cause" and "outer effect" during a conference call between my mother, my sister and myself. The call was regarding property that we had inherited, and, to put it mildly, the call did not go well. I have "latent" athlete's foot, that flares up occasionally as a signal of my well-being (or lack thereof). As soon as I hung up the phone, I felt extremely sharp pains in my toe due to the athletes foot. I hadn't felt this pain prior to the conversation, and I literally limped into my prayer and meditation space. I immediately had to do the emotional release work to find out what was going on. I then had to do prayer and meditation work to still my mind, because I needed to find out where my energy field was not aligned with unconditional love.

Through this process, I recalled an unpleasant event that happened between my sister and myself over 20 years before (I overheard her calling me a fag behind my back and was devastated). I realized that the current situation dredged up those subconscious memories, and the horrible feelings of shame, pain and betrayal that I had carried around for years as a result. I became aware that a part of me felt bad, betrayed, angry and unloved as a result of the situation. I realized that these emotions had little to do with the conversation my sister and I just had (it simply triggered the emotions). I then had to release the emotion, realize that I was not loving myself fully because I felt unworthy, unloved and betrayed as a result of that old event, and then pray that the emotions that were released, be replaced with the truth that I was lovable, worthy and could trust others.

I released the emotion by crying over my feelings of betrayal and unworthiness. I then felt a deep, deep anger that I had carried with me for years that my sister (who I had placed in the role of my protector) would betray me in this way. I released this anger by screaming at my sister "How dare you!!! Finally, I became aware of a deep shame within me that stemmed from this episode. I became aware of this shame, acknowledged it, and felt it moving through me. I then felt the catharsis that comes after having a good cry.

I became aware of the erroneous beliefs that I had held and the emotions that they created (shame, betrayal, anger and rage). These emotions had not moved, but had been forced into a deep level of my consciousness and were reflected in my body, where I had literally forced them down to the tips of my toes. After moving the emotions, the pain of my athlete's foot subsided within fifteen minutes. I had healed my body as a result of healing my mind. Once my mind was healed, I no longer needed to manifest the physical discomfort to "wake me up" to the need to align my thoughts completely with the Simple Truth.

In this example, we also see that prayer was an integral part of the process of transformation. However, prayer is also a concept that is sometimes misunderstood. Prayer is simply "talking to GOD" in the same way that meditation is "listening to GOD." Once we drop the misperceptions that we have about what GOD is and isn't, we can learn to open to the energy of GOD in prayer and meditation in the same way that we open up to a friend who comes over for coffee.

Prayer is simply invoking the power of GOD into a situation, by acknowledging the existence of a higher power.

Through this invocation, you give the "higher power" permission to work on the situation that is being contemplated, and thus you surrender your will to the will of GOD (which is simply that you be happy and fulfilled). Prayer opens your energy field so that the higher power can permeate it more deeply (think of yourself as a transducer for electromagnetic energy that can then be focused on whatever situation is in need of prayer). As you focus more of this energy onto the person or situation, the energy transforms it. As you become adept at this process, your power to transform situations through the use of prayer increases in the same way that your power to lift weights increases as you lift them more often.

Prayer Changes Things. Some examples of specific prayers are listed in Chapter 10 of this book.

So prayer and affirmations can change our minds. Emotional release can change our energy fields and bodies. These activities work in concert to mitigate situations we no longer desire and create situations that are affirming to us. Think of prayer, meditation and affirmations as one side of the coin and the emotional work as the other side of the coin. Our Pathway to Inner Peace is not complete without all of these components. Since emotional release is not well understood, the next chapter offers steps that can be used in the process of release.

Chapter Nine

7-Pathways To Inner Peace

The Final Journey

So how do we do this emotional work? There are seven
steps to the process, and these steps involve everything that
we have discussed so far. We must release our emotions
because any time our emotions flare up, it is a call for healing. When we have an emotional flare-up, we should go into
the safe space that we've created for ourselves through prayer
and meditation. As we meditate, we access the answers and
insights that can help us to transform our minds, which in
turn can help heal our bodies. In our safe space, we can take
The 7 Pathways to Inner Peace.

Pathway 1:
✦ *Have the Emotion* ✦

The first thing we must do when emotions flare up is to
simply be aware of them. Instead of suppressing it, HAVE
THE EMOTION. There may be many reasons that we deny

the emotion. If we're sitting in a business meeting, it's probably not a good idea to stand up and hit someone, so we suppress the urge to do so. We deny the emotion because we should be "in control." We deny the emotion because we "shouldn't" feel that way —

"I'm on a spiritual path and therefore I shouldn't feel anger" // "I shouldn't feel pain." // "I shouldn't feel negation." // "I shouldn't feel these feelings of inadequacy."

We deny the emotions because we were told to. Our programming says big boys don't cry. Our programming says if I am a woman and I rant and rave and scream and rage, then that makes me a raving maniac.

Of course there are times when it is inappropriate and unsafe to have the emotion, but that is why we built a safe space for ourselves for prayer and meditation. In that safe space, we have created a place where GOD's Light can come in to transform the emotion. In that safe space, we have created a place where we understand what triggered the emotion. In that safe space, there is healing power to heal that emotion. So we HAVE THE EMOTION!

Pathway 2:

✦ *Honor the Emotion* ✦

We should HONOR the Emotion, too. Many times we discount our emotions – especially in a male-dominated society where emotions are seen as "female" things. We subjugate them so much that we don't realize that our emotions are just signals. We feel a subconscious shame that compounds the negative impact that the emotion has on our energy field, and thus on our lives. Emotions are really wonderful, divine tools, that signal to us where our thoughts and beliefs are not in alignment with the truth, and therefore do not give us peace. And so, as we understand our emotions, we can see them as wonderful tools that help us get back to the inner peace.

We can choose to see our emotions as road signs that will move us back into alignment with the simple truth. Seeing our emotions in this light also helps us to see them more objectively, and to have a sense of humor about them. We can begin to honor those emotions.

Emotions are seen as something that spiritual people don't and shouldn't have. Emotions are also seen as these nasty, testy little things that cause disruption. However, emotions are seen as disruptive because they have been misused. They have been pent-up for so long that they have caused damage, because when they are finally released, they are released in a torrent of destructiveness due to the sheer volume of emotion that has been suppressed. Imagine a pressure cooker, and the damage that it causes when it explodes. The destructiveness of such a device is like a bomb. Therefore, we must learn to honor the emotion. You must learn that if you are feeling pain, anger or fear that is a part of you that needs nurturing. All of you is good, all of you is acceptable, all of you is lovable, and the "negative" emotion is just a part of your consciousness that doesn't know it yet.

And so this part of you comes up in your mind, this part of you manifests in your body so that you can teach it a new way.

Through prayer and meditation you can shine the light of GOD's unconditional love on it, which lets it know that it is loved. Through prayer and meditation you can give it what it needs and you transform this part of your consciousness. You can transform your consciousness so that little by little, every part of your energy field gets transformed into that which reflects the truth and the light that it is. Through this process, every part of your being gets transformed into a gentle, loving peaceful energy, that has the capacity to attract and retain joy. With this process, every part of your consciousness gets transformed into a reflection of the GOD-Self that it is, and that it was designed to be. So we honor the emotion by being willing to see the emotion in a new way so that we may honor it for its role in our growth.

Step 3:

✦ *Honor Yourself* ✦

We must HONOR our SELVES, which is step three. Many times we want to beat up on ourselves for having the emotion. Big boys don't cry, so I must be a wimp. If I'm a woman, if I rage and scream and shout, and show my anger, then I'm a ranting, raving, bitch. If we are on a spiritual path already and we have these emotions, we feel that we are bad people for having them, because we view the emotions as being bad. Therefore, we must come to the same understanding of ourselves, that we have come to with our emotions. We must understand that our situations are simply "road maps" that show us where we are aligned with the simple truth of GOD's unconditional love, and where we are not. Therefore, we must not judge ourselves for our situation, for it is the perfect one to teach us where to align more closely to the consciousness of GOD.

Although we must not judge ourselves or the situation, we must take responsibility for it because our thoughts and beliefs have created it. However, we must understand that taking responsibility for something is not taking blame for it. Blame connotes that the event is somehow "bad." This judgment need not apply to our situation because we have already established that it is the perfect situation to help us to grow. We did the best that we could when we created the situation based on what we knew then. Now that our consciousness is expanding, we know something different, and we apply this new knowledge to every aspect of our lives. However, we don't punish our selves for what was created out of the old knowledge, because then, we didn't know any better. Now that we know better, we have the power to change, and to heal. We are taking extremely courageous steps in this process of healing, so we should honor ourselves instead of blaming ourselves.

In reviewing the first three steps, after we moved into our safe space: We had the emotion; We honored the emotion; We honored ourselves for having the emotion. Then we move to step Four. Remember this is all done in the context of our safe space, where it is safe and wise to have the emotion.

Step 4:

✦ Release the Emotion ✦

Step Four is the most important step in this process and that is to release the emotion. As you recall, e-motions are simply energy in motion, and what you are doing is releasing the old, stagnant energy out of your energy field. This energy (or these emotions) is repressed fear and anger that you have held. For example, we may believe that we are unworthy of a partner who treats us lovingly. This belief may be ingrained deeply into our consciousness due to unaffirming situations that we have experienced in our lives. This belief may create an experience of frustration for us because we seem unable to attract or retain a loving mate. The situation may cause us to feel angry at the world, ourselves or the other person. We must release these emotions so that we make room for a more evolved view of ourselves that reflects GOD's unconditional love for us, the universe's unconditional support of all that we need, and (most important in this case) our unconditional love for ourselves. As we release the old emotion, we move these old energies out of our energy field so that we no longer draw to us experiences that reflect our lack of love for ourselves and what this lack of love has created. In other words, when you release the old, stagnant energy, you create a vacuum that attracts a more loving experience.

Release the emotion with your mind

There are many ways to release the emotions. One way

is with your mind. This is where the imagination exercises from the previous chapter of this book come in handy. These imagination exercises help us to go back to the situations that created these emotions. We can re-visit them, re-live them, and re-play them. When we go "back there" we re-experience the feelings in a "safe" space where we have power. We can scream, we can cry, we can rage, we can beat our pillows, we can fight our attackers. We can also change the situation and it's outcome. By changing the situation and its outcome, we release from our mind any lasting scars that the situation has left because we begin to see the situation differently.

For example, at one point, I held an old, unaffirming memory of a schoolteacher who told me to sit down and shut up in an extremely forceful way. This memory was buried in my subconscious and made me feel like my contributions to any situation would not be valuable because I was not a valuable person. As a result, I didn't speak up in business meetings, and this arrested my career development. I went back and started visualizing myself talking back to the teacher, affirming my worth, and that my input had value. I also screamed and called her names.

As a result, I regained a confidence that I didn't know that I had lost because a part of my consciousness was transformed from "un-loving" to self-loving.

Release the emotion with your voice

It is also important to use your voice because much of the energy that we have suppressed has been suppressed in our vocal chords. In the prior example, I used my physical voice to "tell the teacher off." The screaming and raging and cussing that you do will release pent-up energy from your energy field and emotional body. You will be surprised by the peace that you feel (and the changes in your physical well-being that you begin to experience) as a result of this process. If you have trouble beginning this process, you can begin using the sound OHM as you think of the situations that cause you emotional pain. When you "tone" the sound OHM with the intention of releasing emotional pain, it is automatically transformed because you are invoking the light of GOD in the process.

Release the Emotion With Your Physical Body

It is also very important to use our physical bodies because so much energy is held there. Many of our memories are imprinted and stored in our bodies. For example, when I was a child, I received a pretty severe beating when I was 7 or 8. I had totally forgotten about this episode with my conscious mind. Almost 30 years later, I was getting a massage, and this memory flooded back into my conscious mind. It was buried in the cells of my body (a phenomena know as cellular memory), and the cells of my body held that imprint until my consciousness was strong enough to release it. Body work such as therapeutic massage, Reiki, Rolfing, energy work and energy healing, can help us to identify those old pains when we are ready to release them. So if we need help identifying these emotions and releasing them, therapeutic energy work can be very useful. You'd be surprised at what type of memories flood in when one is in that state. Because as you submit yourself to this body work, you are in a meditative state.

If you have difficulty releasing emotions physically, you can use intense physical exercise. If we choose to run, we can run out some of the emotions. Simply think of the anger, pain, rage, or fear that you are feeling while engaging in a good run, and you will find that these emotions fuel your exercise in a new and interesting way. The exercise becomes more cathartic and you will be amazed at the amount of energy that you find. Of course you can also use the stairmaster, the exercise bicycle, the rowing machine or whatever health machine is available to you by the time you read this book. Simply focus on the emotion, have the emotion and channel that energy into the effort. Physical exercise may be a very effective way to begin bringing suppressed emotions to the forefront, and like any activity, the more you do it, the easier it will become.

Frantically cleaning your house (as a form of physical exercise) could also be a good way to release pent-up emotions (and can be very productive as well). You'll be surprised at how quickly you become comfortable working with your emotions in this way. Soon you'll be ready to work with your emotions in many other ways in the safe space that you have created for yourself through prayer and meditation.

Other ways that you may work with emotional release are as unlimited as your creativity. You can rant and rave. You can "cuss someone out." You can scream and cry. Beat your pillow. The powers of imagination that you have cultivated are now expanded, so situations from the past that have caused emotional pain are easily brought to your consciousness. These old situations work in concert with the current situations that trigger your emotional release, in a way similar to the example that I used regarding my sister and my athlete's foot. You use your mind, your voice and your body while in a safe, prayerful and meditative space.

When you surrender to this process, you have opened the way for more feelings of unconditional love. A new found peace comes into your energy field and replaces those old grudges that you have just released. Your safe space is a place where you have cultivated an energy of unconditional love through prayer and meditation, so it contains much healing power. Therefore, when you release the emotions, you are already conditioned to absorb that loving energy that would readily replace these dark spaces in your consciousness. Your safe space is certainly a more effective forum for releasing pent-up emotions, not only because you will not harm or disrupt others (or yourself), but also because you can readily replace the energy with the energy of light (unconditional love) that has been established in your safe space. The energy of light brings with it peace, comfort and the ability to attract and sustain joy.

You already know this. You already know that peaceful feeling that washes over you after you've had a good cry. That peaceful feeling is simply the unconditional love replacing the grief that's been released through crying. So, in the safe space we have the emotion. And when this peaceful feeling descends on us, more of GOD's infinite intelligence also descends on us, and carries with it the information that will help us to heal our perceptions further. When this information descends on us we are able to take the next step.

Step 5:

✦ *Ask* ✦
(To understand the root cause of the issue)

The awareness that breaks through your consciousness has answers for you. You should ask:

"What is this situation truly about?"

———

"What has caused this situation?"

———

"What is the misperception that I carry in my energy field and in my belief system, that has caused me to create the situation that has caused me pain?"

You will then become aware of the answer.

We can create an unlimited number of situations that will show us our thought patterns (and where they are aligned or not aligned with the "simple truth"). However, regardless of the situation, we will come to the following conclusion about it:

1. This is a place where I believed that GOD did not love me completely and unconditionally;

2. This is a place where I did not believe that the universe supports me completely and unconditionally;

3. This is a place where I am not loving myself completely and unconditionally.

Because the "sponsoring thought" was not consistent with these simple truths, the experiences that caused pain, suffering, fear, anger (which is fear turned outward), depression (which is anger turned inward) or deprivation. Our experiences are just as varied and unique as we are. However, the root causes of these situations are very uniform – these beliefs (or "sponsoring thoughts") are not consistent with the "3 simple truths":

1. *GOD loves us completely and unconditionally.*
2. *The universe supports us completely and unconditionally.*
3. *We love ourselves completely and unconditionally.*

For example, sitting in traffic is one of the most annoying aspects of urban and suburban life. You may ask yourself why does traffic cause such an emotional reaction that may range from mild irritation to potentially fatal "road rage." Your first response might be "I am going to be late for work." At a deep level, you may believe that you will be punished for being late, which is based on the misperception that there is a force outside of you (a surrogate for GOD) that would punish you because subconsciously you believe that GOD punishes. This misperception is inconsistent with the truth that GOD loves you completely and unconditionally.

At a deeper level, you may also believe that traffic will always screw up your life, which reflects the misperception that the universe does not support you. This is inconsistent with the truth that the universe supports you completely and unconditionally. At a deep level you may also believe that you deserve this inconvenience, which reflects a lack of love for yourself. The truth is that you have permission to love yourself completely and unconditionally. Regardless of the outer situation, and what emotions are brought up as a result, the situation reflects a deeper mis-alignment with the Simple Truth.

Knowing that the situations that we create are simply "guideposts" to show us where we are (or where we are not) aligned with the simple truths, it is easier for us to see all our situations as simple tools of our own invention. These tools help us toward our ultimate goal of spiritual growth and development, and the objective of spiritual growth and development is so that we experience the bliss and peace that comes from re-aligning our thoughts (and thus our experiences) with the divine. Therefore, we no longer have to judge our experiences, or blame others for them. We simply use them as tools, and find them to be as harmless as a garden rake. We observe and release the emotions that they trigger, and once we have found the peace that follows release, we ask "what misperception has caused me to create this situation?"

We will get the answer through our meditations (we have become very adept at getting insights from the infinite intelligence through the discipline of meditation). We now know the erroneous belief (or sponsoring thought) that we have to transform. Therefore we are ready to take the next step.

Pathway 6:

✦ *Pray for a Miracle* ✦
(And expect that you will receive it)

When we become aware of the misperception that has created the difficult situation, we pray, "Mother-Father GOD, I have held a misperception in my mind. I have held energy regarding that misperception in my body. I have created difficult situations for myself based on this misperception. I have now released the energy created by this old perception so I pray that you remove this old perception from my mind, my body and my affairs. I pray for a shift in my perception. I pray that this shift in my perception occur so that I no longer have to create experiences based on that old and erroneous belief or thought."

Before the New Age, we prayed for forgiveness of our "sins." Our new understanding is that "sin" is simply thoughts or actions that are inconsistent with the Simple Truth. Because these thoughts are inconsistent with the simple truth, they bring about situations that seem painful.

We learned that the wages of sin was death. Through our new understanding we learn that this death does not come from a hateful, vengeful and punitive GOD, but through having beliefs that are not aligned with the truth. These "killing thoughts" create situations that "kill off" our ability to experience ourselves as divine, innocent, loving, lovable children of GOD, because we "kill off" our ability to experience our connection with the divine. Therefore, a "figurative" death occurs instead of "literal" death. As we have a new understanding of sin, we understand that by aligning our beliefs, thoughts and actions with the truth brings us peace, prosperity, and integration with our spiritual selves or our higher selves, and therefore integration with more of GOD energy. Therefore, we pray for a release from erroneous, unaligned thinking. We pray for a shift, so that we no longer have those erroneous perceptions that cause pain, grief, anger, fear, and rage. Instead, we pray for the perception that creates joy and love and harmony and all that is good. We pray for the perception that GOD loves us completely and unconditionally, the universe supports us completely and unconditionally, and that we love ourselves completely and unconditionally. And as we pray, we pray for that miracle. That miracle that is a shift in our perception.

We must also Expect the Miracle. Many times when we pray, we say the words but we don't really believe it. Somehow, subconsciously we still believe that GOD would withhold our desires. We affirm the words but we don't really believe them. We still believe that the universe doesn't support our desires, or we believe that we don't deserve our desires because we don't love ourselves completely and unconditionally. We may hold images from the past in our mind when what we wanted has not come to us. We may hold images from the past where we have been frustrated, or where we have not been loved. We hold these images from the past because that is what we know (and can relate to) with our human mind. Unfortunately that past, and the imprint that it has left, attracts that same thing to us again because we emit that vibration and attract its reflection.

We have given the past power over us. We can use the affirmation "The Past Has No Power Over Me!" to begin releasing these self-imposed limitations. We can use the power and creativity that we have developed in our creative space to envision and create new experiences. These new experiences are not based on the past. They are based on the glorious present and the glorious future that we create as the light of GOD shines on us in our prayerful and meditative space. We can pray that the imprinting from the past be removed from our consciousness, and thus we create with expectation, based on our new understandings. The removal of our past imprinting and the shift in our perception that results is the "miracle" for which we pray.

To illustrate praying with expectancy, I will share a story about a man who plays the Lottery. The man affirmed that he was going to win the lottery a million times. The man visualized himself winning the lottery. He prayed that he would win the lottery. However, every day when he went to check his numbers, when he found out that he didn't "hit the numbers," he'd say "I knew I wasn't going to win." Somewhere within him he wasn't expecting a miracle. He did all the right things and he mouthed all the right words. However, he didn't go forward with expectation. And this thwarted his ability to create lottery winnings. So, EXPECT A MIRACLE! Expect that the shift in perception will occur, and that this shift in your perception will enable you to create what you desire (and remove that which you no longer need or can learn from).

My personal experience with creating my "miracles" comes from my adolescence. There was a song entitled "Good Morning Heartache" from the movie, "Lady Sings The Blues" based on the life of Billie Holliday. For years in the seventies and the eighties I would wake up singing that song. The lyrics were as follows:

Good morning heartache, you old a gloomy sight.
Good morning heartache, thought you said good-bye last night.
I tossed and turned 'til it seemed that you had gone,
but here you are with the dawn.
Wish I could forget you, but you're here to stay.
It seems I met you when my love went away.
Now every-day I start by saying to you,
good morning heartache, what's new?

Those lyrics were part of my core of creativity. Those lyrics made up part of my "sponsoring thoughts," and I was creating based on that premise. I was extremely successful creating on this premise, so when I came to this understanding, I prayed for a miracle. I prayed for a shift in my perception that this no longer be a part of my sponsoring thought patterns. With much prayer and much release and much work, it occurred to me one day that it had been months — and then it occurred to me that it had been years since I woke up singing "Good Morning Heartache."

My perception had shifted. My mind had changed. The dirt had been cleared from my mental dirtbag, the kinks had been removed from my garden hose, and the impurities had been cleared from my fuel tank. The energy of change had washed over my mind and my body and my affairs, where no cell in my body was holding the thought or the belief or the experience of HEARTACHE any more. So I expected the miracle and the miracle occurred. And it will occur for you!

Pathway 7:

✦ *Rinse and Repeat* ✦

The next step, or the seventh, is called Rinse and Repeat. You generally find these instructions on shampoo bottles, and it encourages you to use more shampoo (much to the delight of the major shampoo manufactuers). In this case I mean that you must use this process as much as necessary in your life to move you to a place of inner peace. Many times our experiences have run so deep and have left such a lasting imprint on us, that it is not possible to banish all unaffirming thoughts, actions and beliefs in one or two sessions. It has taken a long, long, time to develop our current consciousness. It may take a while to dissolve it as well because it has been so deeply ingrained. Therefore, we must continually apply the 7 Pathways, for all the situations in our lives. We may not always need to go "by the book" in applying the 7 Steps, but by using the process dynamically as we need to, we can release our old emotional baggage.

At first it may seem difficult because our lives may seem to get a little more confused than they already are. However, that is because we have opened to a shift and so what we are doing is now creating situations that will give us the opportunity to shift. We are creating situations that give us the opportunity to see our beliefs and to HEAL them. We can now see our emotions and HEAL them. We can now see our perceptions and HEAL them. So we continually apply this process to anything in our experiences that triggers us into emotional release.

We will create some doozies! However as we continually

apply this process, we get better at applying it, in the same way that we play the piano better when we practice our scales. The more we practice, the better we get. And because our consciousness is like an onion, we begin to peel back the layers of our consciousness.

What we find is that our list of "issues" is not endless, they are simply the same core issues repeated over and over in different situations. We may see an endless array of misperceptions, but the more we peel the onion, the closer we get to the core. And just like an onion, the closer we get to the core the sweeter it becomes. As you know, when you begin to peel an onion, there may be tears, but as you get to the sweet core, the tears subside.

For example, as I started my life, I experienced the deep lack that comes from being economically disadvantaged. This lack was a reflection of a part of my consciousness that didn't believe that the universe supported me completely and unconditionally. As I evolved and healed my perceptions, I started to experience more abundance, and the fear and pain of being in lack began to subside. I had begun to learn the lesson that all that I needed was given to me by the universe (GOD's creation), which supports me completely and unconditionally. However, the misperception that I would (or should) live in lack was deeply ingrained, so I repeatedly had to learn the lesson over and over again by experiencing feelings of lack and transforming them.

Several years ago, I had to take a 6 foot pile of newspapers up to the street for recycling. This was not an easy task because my driveway is about 100 yards uphill and it was a blisteringly hot, humid summer day. After complaining and moaning; huffing and puffing to take the papers up a little at a time, my cleanly pressed shirt was completely soaked, my suit looked like I had slept in it, and I was running late for my business appointment. As I backed my car out of the clearing I had made in the garage, I looked over and saw a little red dolly (the kind used to carry washers, dryers, boxes and piles of newspaper). I couldn't believe it, so I asked "what was the lesson I was to learn from this." The answer I received was quite clear – that all that I needed would always be provided to me by the universe.

This situation was clearly not life threatening, was simply resolved, and only caused a minor inconvenience. However, I still needed to shift my consciousness at an even deeper level. Some time later, I was looking for a tape recorder to record a counseling session, and I looked everywhere (becoming frustrated and running behind in my commitments as a result). The next day, I found the tape recorder exactly where it always was, on a shelf directly behind my chair. It had been there all along in the most obvious place. When I asked what lesson I was to learn from this experience, the answer was again the same – that all that I needed would always be provided to me by the universe. However, this time, the lesson was an even more innocuous situation, because the deeper parts of my consciousness that still held a belief in lack were easily transformed due to my continually expanding awareness. You will also find that your "lessons" become increasingly innocuous as your awareness expands.

Your awareness will expand to the point where you create a lesson in a little thing like finding a parking space. Or you get a lesson in a little thing like a small and innocent loving interaction with another individual as opposed to these huge situations such as the Big Bangs that I referred to earlier, like divorce, loss of a job, loss of a relationship, loss of a loved one, etc. So we rinse and repeat.

The techniques I have described have also helped others. One person that I have worked with suffered a series of "big bangs" that literally broke her heart. Within the space of a year, she had lost her mother, her job, and her financial security. She was angry, hurt and terrified because the very foundations of her identity had been called into question. Through the process of emotional release, opening to new truths about her life and her "true" identity (which had nothing to do with her "false-ego"), and through the transformative power of prayer and meditation, she was able to heal her broken heart. Within a year she had manifested several new professional opportunities as a freelancer that gave her renewed financial abundance. However, this new abundance was simply the Outer Effect of the Inner Cause (she found a deeper level of Inner Peace and more self love, and this was reflected in her outer world).

Another person I have worked with had become emotionally closed off (due to experiences in her past where she continually suffered criticism). She had built a shell of "hardened energy" around her energy field to protect her from what she perceived to be a hostile universe. In the words of a recent song by Madonna, she was frozen and her heart had difficulty opening. By opening to the loving energy of the universe in prayer and meditation, and releasing the old, hardened emotions, she was able to "break out of her shell" and experience more joy and freedom than she ever thought possible.

The technique that you have just read about is very useful in moving your emotions, and thus clearing your energy field. However, it is also important to understand your emotions more fully. Although you may experience a whole range of emotions, it might be easier to see the array of emotions in one of two categories — those emotions that reflect love, and those emotions that reflect fear. Emotions that reflect love are used to show us where we are vibrating with the unconditional love of GOD. Examples are the joyous anticipation that a child has before Christmas (or that we have prior to a big event), joy, peace, exhilaration, and of course love.

Emotions that reflect fear are used to show us where we are not aligned with the unconditional love of GOD. Examples are anger, rage (which is an expression of anger), depression (which is anger turned inward), procrastination (which is immobility due to fear), and of course fear itself.

Fear has many faces. Other faces of fear include hatred, hubris, divisiveness, defensiveness, paranoia, exploitation, dishonesty and denial.

Let's talk about the "key" emotions that we feel. Anger! Anger is based on fear and is an outward expression of fear. Somehow, we feel that something vital for our survival is being withheld from us, and so we feel threatened. The child within us perceives that its needs (which have been transferred onto the current situation) will not be met. As a result, we react in anger. We understand that all that we need comes from within us, because we create it. As we remember our connection with GOD, we understand that GOD would not withhold anything from us. We understand that GOD is not a punitive being, but is a force that wants to give us all that we can accept.

As we come to this new understanding, we are able to release our anger, for we no longer have fear of GOD's retribution. We no longer have fear that something we need for our survival will elude us. And therefore we can express our anger, release it and transform it, and open to more and more of GOD's love and bounty.

Guilt is a very pervasive and insidious emotion. We carry memories of our "transgressions" in this life, and we also carry memories of our "transgressions" in prior realms of existence. These subconscious feelings are like invisible weights that keep us from feeling the buoyancy of light that wants to manifest through us and raise our vibrations to lift us to a higher level of existence. Guilt originated from our perception that we are separate from GOD the source. We misunderstand that as we emanated from GOD the source as an individualized expression of GOD, that we became less than the source, and therefore less worthy of love and less whole. This misunderstanding has been compounded through eons of experience that have been created as a result of this misunderstanding.

We have forgotten that it was created as an individualized expression of GOD, so that the light of GOD could expand, create and thus be magnified. We erroneously believe that we have moved away from the source. Therefore we feel the guilt of an errant child, and believe that simple acts of expression are "transgressions."

I recently observed guilt in action when visiting an elderly friend in a nursing home. My friend's roommate had a son who was well-to-do and powerful in life. Apparently he was also very busy because he visited his mother quite infrequently (even though he lived close by). However, every time he visited, he raised holy hell about his mother's care. He terrified, bullied and harangued the staff like your typical playground bully. However, through the bravado, what became clear to me (and others) was that he was overcompensating for his feelings of guilt regarding his mother.

Guilt is useless. Nothing will change the past. At any given point each one of us is doing the best we can with what we know at any given time. We have never really left the "Garden of GOD's Love." We have remained the beautiful flowers of that garden, and our task now is to remind ourselves of this truth. In this truth we are innocent – not guilty. In this truth we are perfect – not flawed. A large part of this process is remembering this truth, and thus remembering who we truly are – individual expressions of GOD's love.

Depression, or any form of self-rejection, is anger or fear turned inward. Once again, we fear that something vital for our survival will be withheld from us and as a result we turn our anger inward toward ourselves. We make ourselves vulnerable to the effects of self-rejection and self-hatred and these energies slow our vibration. These energies keep us from attracting our desires to us and actually attract events that would cause us pain. As we go through our lives, we exude an energy that reflects our feelings about ourselves. Many times, that energy is like a sign on our backs that tells the universe "Kick Me." Just like when someone places a "Kick Me" sign on your back in grammar school, the universe responds to the invisible "Kick Me" sign and you wonder why the Universe keeps kicking you.

As we come to a new understanding of GOD's unconditional love for us, we can no longer turn our anger inward to create painful situations in our lives. We can take the invisible "Kick Me" sign off our backs. We can reverse it, so that we send a signal to the universe that says "Kiss Me" in the same way that you reverse the sign on a unisex bathroom as you enter it. The choice is always ours, so we must continually monitor our thoughts and ask ourselves "am I sending a "Kick Me" or a "Kiss Me" signal to the Universe. As we feel GOD's complete and unconditional love coursing through our bodies in prayer and meditation, it becomes inconceivable for us to reject ourselves, because we feel GOD's love moving through us. It becomes inconceivable for us to fear GOD withholding anything from us, because we feel GOD simply as the infinite, powerful, all-loving life force expressing through us. And therefore we no longer have need for depression. We release it and we raise our vibration to the state that is it's natural state. A vibration of buoyancy, expansion and unconditional Love.

At first you may find it difficult to trace the outer reason for your emotional state to the root cause (your key misperception). You can do this by continually asking yourself "why" you feel a certain way. In the previous example, when asking why being stuck in traffic made you angry and anxious, you eventually came to the root cause (your erroneous belief) that the universe didn't support you. You may also have a fear that you will be punished (for being late) or that something that you need for your survival (a paycheck) might be withheld from you.

In this situation, you may also feel threatened because the fear of being late makes you less than perfect, whole or complete, and therefore fills you with a sense of shame. You may subconsciously tie your sense of self-worth to your ability to get to your destination on time, and when things that you can't control happen, your sense of self-worth is threatened. I call any event that threatens your sense of self-worth a "self-quake" because it feels like the event will "rock your world." A "self-quake" is the most common event that can "trigger" an emotional release.

Subconsciously, you may derive some portion of your self worth from the way others see you, the way your spouse treats you, or from the actions of others. You cannot control any of these things, because all individuals have free will. However, when your sense of self-worth is dependent on the views or actions of others, you have an "investment" in their views or actions. A job assignment or any event that you are responsible for are just a couple of examples of times when the way others see you (your investment) is put "at risk."

When we feel that there is something outside of ourselves (and our connection with GOD) that gives us what we need to survive, we may have a "self-quake" that triggers emotional release. In truth, the child that continues to live within us, has transferred his need for his parents' love and acceptance onto the current situation. Remember, from the perspective of this child, he must have his parents' approval in order to get what he needs to survive. Therefore, on a conscious level, an innocuous situation may trigger a deep, primal fear of pain, suffering and death.

These strong emotions cause "self-quakes." In the example of being stuck in traffic, we see how cases of "road rage" may occur.

If you continually ask "why am I feeling threatened," you will get to the root cause that created your "self-quake." You will find that your "false ego" feels threatened. As you move through your process of growth, your "false ego" will come out in many ways because it fears that it is being destroyed. The "false ego" does not realize that it is not being destroyed or eviscerated, that it is simply being transformed so that it can no longer lead you into pain or suffering. It is being replaced by your true identity as a beloved, innocent and perfect child of GOD, and this new identity would lead you into peace and joy and bliss. Therefore, you must become your "thought police" and observe your thoughts and your reactions to the things that happen to you in your world. The events in your life will indicate your inner consciousness and trigger you into emotional release when there is an erroneous belief that it is time to transform. The prayers in the next chapter will outline the key misperceptions that are at the "root cause" of your emotional state.

As we recognize all our emotions as either love or fear (the absence of love) we can use the following wisdom to help conquer our fears:

The process of eliminating fear begins with your mind. First you must know that there is a power, an energy and a great love that supports, sustains, protects, and nurtures you. You may perceive this energy to be outside of you. However, as you experience this energy through your prayers and meditations, the channel between you and this energy (that you perceive outside of you) becomes stronger.

As you work with this energy more and more, you feel more physical manifestations of this energy working with you physically, and in every aspect of your life. This energy permeates deeper levels of your consciousness, until it BECOMES your consciousness.

You can help this process through your prayers and meditations by saying to the energy that surrounds you (which is the energy of GOD) "I am afraid. I am afraid of .... (list your fears). You may release your fears in any way that you find appropriate, including stating them, screaming them, or moaning. By releasing the fear, you make room for a new energy.

As you invite this extremely powerful energy into your energy field, it takes those fears and transforms them, moves them out, and replaces them with a feeling of peace and security. This is the peace that passes all understanding. When you are vibrating in this peace you can only create reflections of this peace.

Do not deny your fears, for that will not release you from them. You do not have to be ashamed of them — they are an illusion. As you work to release your fears they will be taken from you.

You may repeat the following prayer:

Mother Father GOD, please release me from my fears. My fears do not give me peace, and your will for me is to have peace. My will for me is to have peace. I align my will with your will. I give you permission to heal my mind, my body and my affairs. I give you permission to remove anything from my energy field that would cause me fear. I ask that I know only your peace. I cast my fears upon the water, like crumbs of bread that get lost in the infinite ocean of your love. They are dissolved by the infinite power of your love, so I release my fears to you.

Know that GOD is with you always. Know that GOD supports you. Know that GOD affirms you when others seem not to. Know of your goodness. Know of your graciousness. Know of your strength. Know of your brilliance. Know of your ability. You do not have to apologize to anyone. You do not have to feel less than anyone. You do not have to have fear, for the light of GOD within you is brilliant, and powerful, and creative, and resourceful, and strong and masterful. Know that these descriptors also describe you.

The prayer that you have just read is one of many in your continuing Pathways To Inner Peace. The next chapter outlines a number of specific prayers that you can use to speed your journey.

Pathways to Inner Peace

Chapter Ten

The Power of Prayer
and
Personal Ritual

A Song and a Prayer Rules

As you see from the 7 Pathways to Inner Peace, Prayer was an integral part of the process. In fact, Prayer is so integral to the process of personal transformation that focusing on prayer individually is warranted. Prayer Changes Things. Prayer acknowledges and invokes the power of GOD and gives that power the permission to work on a situation.

We must give the energy of GOD permission to work on a situation because we have created these situations out of free will, and we retain that free will. Therefore by acknowledging and invoking the power of GOD, we give that power permission to transform us.

Prayer helps to shift our minds, and helps us to change our beliefs and what we create with our beliefs. Just as there is no right or wrong way to meditate, there is no right or wrong way to pray. As you become more comfortable with prayer (and your personal relationship with the energy of GOD) your prayers may begin to resemble a conversation that you might have with a trusted friend who loves you completely and unconditionally.

Below I have listed some additional prayers that can be used for specific emotions that you encounter on your Pathway To Inner Peace.

A Prayer For Addressing Fear

Mother/Father – GOD; I have fear. I express this fear now. This fear is based on misperceptions. The misperception is that you do not love me. The misperception is that the universe does not support me. The misperception is that I am not lovable and worthy. I ask for a miracle. I ask that you heal my mind of this misperception now! I ask that my mind be filled with the truth that you love me completely and unconditionally. I ask to be filled with the truth that the universe supports me completely and unconditionally. I ask to be filled with the truth that I am perfect and innocent and therefore lovable. With this truth I ask for healing of my mind, my body, and my affairs, so that the fear and the effects of the fear are no longer evident in my life. AMEN.

A Prayer For Surrender

Mother/Father – GOD; Today I surrender to your Holy Spirit for healing, wholeness and peace. I surrender my

FEAR. I cast my fear upon the water like bread crumbs on the ocean. My fears dissolve in the infinite ocean of GOD's Unconditional Love. I surrender my ANGER. My anger is simply fear that your love is withheld from me. This is an illusion, and I move through the illusion now and surrender my fear to the Holy Spirit of GOD. The Holy Spirit transforms my anger into joy. I surrender my TURMOIL. My turmoil is outside of me and outside of my control. I look within and find the peace of GOD within. This changes my outer world and transforms the turmoil into peace. I surrender my EGO. My ego would keep me in pain and suffering. My GOD self would guide me to peace. I surrender my ego to my god self. I surrender my WEAKNESS. My human self feels small, blocked, vulnerable and disconnected from the light of GOD. My GOD self IS the power of GOD. I surrender the illusion of my weakness to the infinite power of GOD. I SURRENDER ALL TO GOD.

A Prayer For Attracting Our Desires

Mother/Father – GOD; I have carried a misperception. The misperception that I have held is that I do not deserve my heart's desires. I ask you to heal that misperception. I ask you to align my thinking with the truth that you want me to have all that I desire. Your will for me is to be happy and fulfilled and complete and whole. For only when I am complete and whole can I fulfill my task on Earth, which is to reflect your light, power, and creativity, and to explore all that I can create as a reflection of you. I open to this truth and therefore I accept fulfillment in the form of my desires. My desires flow to me easily. And so it is! AMEN.

A Prayer For Healing Anger

Mother/Father – GOD; I feel so angry. I release this anger now. I open to a new understanding of this anger. I understand that this anger is based on the misperception that you do not love me. I understand that this anger is based on the misperception that love from others is withheld from me. I understand that this anger is based on the fear that the love that is withheld from me will somehow damage me. Therefore I release this misperception. I ask for you to heal this misperception, by shifting my mind. I ask for the miracle. I expect the miracle that I now come to a new understanding – the understanding that you love me completely and unconditionally – the understanding that the universe supports me completely and unconditionally – the understanding that I am innocent and perfect and therefore lovable. And so it is! AMEN.

A Prayer For Healing

Mother/Father – GOD; I ask that your Holy Spirit heal my mind, body and affairs completely. I ask that your Holy Spirit release me from my traumas of the past. I ask that the self-hatred of the false-ego be dissolved and that it be replaced with the everlasting, unconditional loving acceptance of my eternal soul. AMEN.

A Prayer For Self Acceptance

Mother/Father – GOD; I ask that your Holy Spirit completely heal my mind, body and affairs. I ask for a shift in my perception of myself. Help me to understand completely who I am. I am your beloved and innocent creation. As such, I have the qualities that you have. I am innocent and perfect. Help me to realize that everything I am seeking through others I ALREADY HAVE. Help me to let go of my judgment of myself based on the Earth's flawed consciousness. Help me to love and accept myself completely and unconditionally as you accept me completely and unconditionally. AMEN.

A Prayer For Shifting Perceptions About GOD

Mother/Father – GOD; I fear that you would not support me. I fear that you would withhold from me. I feel that you would punish me. In my human mind, I know this is in error. Therefore I ask you to shift my perception. I surrender my fear of you. I surrender through my voice by expressing it. I surrender through my body by moving the fear through my body. I ask you to transform it so that I create with expectancy what I desire. I look not to people, places or events for the satisfaction of my desires. I look only to you, who will work through an infinite number of people, places and events to ensure that I have what I need. AMEN.

A Prayer For Opening To Abundance

Mother/Father – GOD; my creator and sustainer. I open myself to the truth of my unlimited abundance. I open myself to the truth that nothing would be withheld from me. I open myself to the truth that your will for me is to be happy and fulfilled, for only when I am happy and fulfilled, can I fulfill the divine plan for my life, which is simply to magnify your light, your infinite creativity, and your infinite abundance by exploring, creating, and experimenting with it. I accept this joyous task here and now, knowing that as I expand I also help others to expand. AMEN.

A Prayer For Forgiveness

Mother/Father – GOD; my true desire is union with the light and energy that emanates from your heart. This energy is an energy of peace. In order to open to this peace, I release anything that will not give me peace. Therefore, I am ready to forgive my past traumas, torments and troubles. I forgive those who were involved in my dramas from the past and I thank them for their gifts. The gifts that others have given me have been divine, because they have led me to this space, where I seek union with your heart. Therefore, I bless them, forgive them, and release them as I release myself from my past, and the need to re-create additional dramas based on erroneous thoughts that I now release. I now accept peace. And so it is. AMEN.

A Prayer For Unleashing Creativity

Mother/Father – GOD; I understand that I am your creation. I understand that the spark of light within me that grows daily, is a part of your creativity. I open to this infinite creativity now. I open to this Infinite creativity expressing through my life in every way. And I bring this Infinite creativity to the situation as I desire it. AMEN.

A Prayer For Opening To Wisdom

Mother/Father – GOD; I open to a new perception of myself. I open to the perception of myself that I am your Light in manifestation. Your Light contains all wisdom. I open to the truth that I now contain all wisdom. As I open to this wisdom it expresses through me in wonderful ways. And it heals the situation and applies wisdom to the situation that I am currently in. And so it is! AMEN.

A Prayer For Opening To Peace

Mother/Father – GOD; I open to the peace of knowing of your presence in every aspect of my life. This peace calms my mind, my body and my affairs. It gives me comfort; it gives me assurance. I open to this peace now and I ask it to descend on me. And I accept it as the natural state. Therefore I ask for a miracle. I ask for a shift in my perception so I understand my natural state is to be at peace. My natural state is to be at harmony. My natural state is to be at one with your unconditional love. AMEN.

A Prayer For Releasing Guilt

Mother/Father – GOD; I ask to be released from my past, for it no longer has power over me. I am now creating with my new consciousness, which you are transforming. Therefore, I am willing to come to a new awareness of my past. It has taught me many things. It has given me many things. I now know that I did the best I could with what I knew then. However, my past has no power over me. I am now doing the best that I can with my new awareness. I have patience with myself because I love myself completely and unconditionally.

Therefore, I release guilt from my energy field. I give the Holy Spirit of GOD permission to remove all traces of guilt from me so that I can live with the peace that passes all understanding. This is my divine birthright, and this is my will for myself. And so it is! AMEN.

A Prayer For Healing Relationships

Mother/Father – GOD; I understand that I am seeing reflections of myself in every person and situation in my life. I am seeing reflections that I would judge and find unacceptable. I see these things as unacceptable because I perceive that you see parts of me as unacceptable. I perceive that you judge me. I now know that this is false. You do not judge me in any way. You only love me. You created me in your image. You are light, so I am light. You are perfect and full. Therefore, I am perfect and in no way am I lacking. Therefore, I no longer need to judge any aspect of my consciousness that is reflected to me, and I need not judge myself or others. I ask for peace. I expect peace. I create peace. I accept peace. I have peace. I am peace. And so it is! AMEN.

A Prayer For Releasing Envy

Mother/Father – GOD; I am envious of another person's situation. In my mind I know that envy is a misperception. In my mind I know that envy is based on the false perception that you favor someone more than you favor me. In my mind I fear that I will suffer because I am not in your favor. Therefore, I ask you to heal my mind of these misperceptions. I ask you to heal my mind so that I know only of your unconditional love for all that has been created. I ask that I realize your unconditional love for me, and that you would not withhold that love from me. I ask that I realize my perfection, my equality and my worthiness. I ask that I release the fear that you would withhold anything from me so that I may accept my birthright, which is your bounty. As I accept my bounty, I release my envy of others. As I release my envy of others, I truly know that what is GOD's belongs to everyone. What is GOD's belongs to me and is my due. And so it is! AMEN.

A Prayer For Opening To Joy

Mother/Father – GOD; I release any perception that joy must be accompanied by suffering. I release any desire to learn the lesson of unconditional love through pain and suffering. I open to a new way of living. I open to a new way of believing. I believe that all I desire is given to me. I believe that you love me completely and unconditionally. Therefore, I believe that you would not punish me or make me suffer. I believe that your will for me is to be happy and fulfilled. I believe that your will for me is to have everything and to do everything and to be everything that I desire. This is your truth, and in this truth we are truly your reflection, your power, your infinity and your grace. I give the ocean of light that is your infinity permission to wash over me and heal my mind so that I live in joy. AMEN.

A Prayer For Everything

GOD HELP ME

AMEN

Rituals

Rituals provide a framework for your prayers. By framing your prayers with songs, chants, affirmations and meditation, you solidify and amplify your intent to heal. As result, you create a greater space for the healing to occur in the same way that the "trappings" of a wedding ceremony amplify the importance of the exchanging of vows. Without the ceremony, a wedding would take 5 minutes and would be a dry legal affair. Perhaps this is why rituals in traditional religions are so powerful.

However, as you forge your individual link with GOD, you may choose to create your own rituals based on your specific need at any given time. One of the integral parts of your ritual could be the 7 Pathways To Inner Peace. You might amplify taking these steps by surrounding them with songs that are relevant and have meaning for you, and prayers that are relevant for your intent. I have attached a ritual that might help you create more abundance in your life. I developed this specific ritual when it became apparent to me that issues of accepting my divine gifts were standing between me and my prosperity. This is just one of many examples of rituals that you can develop and use (in your safe space of prayer and meditation) to minister to your own spiritual needs.

VISUALIZATION CEREMONY

Opening: Statement of Purpose:
"Invoking Vision"

Opening Song: *"Bringing In The Sheaves"*

Opening Prayer: Opening Prayer:
"A Prayer For Creativity"

Second Song: *"Great Is Thy Faithfulness"*

Inspirational Reading: Process:
"Creating the Present Perfect":

Write Creations

�֍

State Creations
through Affirmations

�֍

Visualize Creations

✖

Emotionalize Creations

✖

Live the Creations

✖

Note Doubts or Fears

✖

Release Doubts or Fears

✖

Re-Live the Creation

Song: *"This Little Light"*

Prayer of Thanksgiving: *"Re-State Creations"*

Hymn of Hope: *"God's Love, The Light of The World"*

Closing Prayer: *"I Surrender"*

I usually begin my personal rituals by stating my intention. Stating your intention to the Universe in an unequivocal way marshals all the help that you have in the Universe to satisfy your intention. Remember that ambiguous inputs yield ambiguous results.

I then use songs or prayers that have meaning to me to open myself (and the space) to the divine energy that I am invoking as a part of my ritual. Songs also raise my vibrational rate (you vibrate more when you emit sounds, and if you don't think so, just remember how your ears used to vibrate after you left a disco or a rock concert). An increased vibration makes you more consistent with and therefore more receptive to a higher level of divine energy. Sometimes I customize the words to songs in my rituals to suit my purposes. For example, in the ritual I illustrated, I changed the song "Jesus The Light of the World" to "God's Love, The Light of the World" so that my space would be opened to the healing and transformative power of ALL the Ascended Masters (including Buddha, Allah, Krishna etc.) in addition to the Ascended Master Jesus.

Many times I'll find (and read aloud) an inspirational reading relevant to my purpose. Many times these readings will be from texts such as The Lamsa Translation of the Bible, (which eliminates many of the Bible's distortions) A Course In Miracles, or work by others such as Louise Hay. Many times I'll also use my own channeled work from my book *"Channeled Messages From The Masters,"* which is the basis for many of the spiritual truths found in this book.

I then move into a more contemplative state and begin a meditation. In this state, I ask questions (such as those listed in the example ritual that I shared with you) and I receive and react to the answers. You might note that the 7 Pathways To Inner Peace are an integral part of this ritual. This is truly the core of the transformative process that I describe. When this process is finished, I seal it with songs, prayers and thankfulness for the transformation that has occurred.

There are as many rituals as there are situations that you would like to transform. Therefore, you can choose one area of your life and create your own ritual to transform that situation. Many people find the structure of a personal ritual to be comforting. Remember that just as with Prayer and Meditation, there is no right or wrong way to conduct your personal ritual. Whatever works for you is that which is for your greatest good.

These rituals can be done privately. However, many people find comfort in group rituals (and the power of prayer and meditation is increased exponentially as more are gathered in prayer). Therefore, you can also find a place of worship that supports your expanding consciousness.

Guided Meditations

Guided meditations can be an important part of your personal spiritual journey because they help you to visualize what you desire, and visualization is the first step to creating your desires. I have included examples of some guided meditations for your use on your ongoing journey. These guided meditations begin by establishing a feeling of peace and comfort, and then take you through a process to help you deal with issues in your life. Of course you can develop more of your own guided meditations as you move forward, based on your own desires.

Meditation for Protection and Healing

This meditation will help you build your safe space and will establish the discipline to help you move into your safe space. Once you have established this discipline, you will be able to move to a feeling of being in your "safe space" immediately, and this will give you peace and protection as you move through your daily life.

Once you have built your safe space, you can do ANYTHING. I have included several meditations to help with specific processes in your life. However, each of these meditations should be preceded by either a meditation for peace and protection, followed by the journey to your safe space. Once you become adept at drawing to you the peace and protection that you desire, you can do so immediately and move through a transformative meditation very quickly.

Begin by taking a deep, deep breath

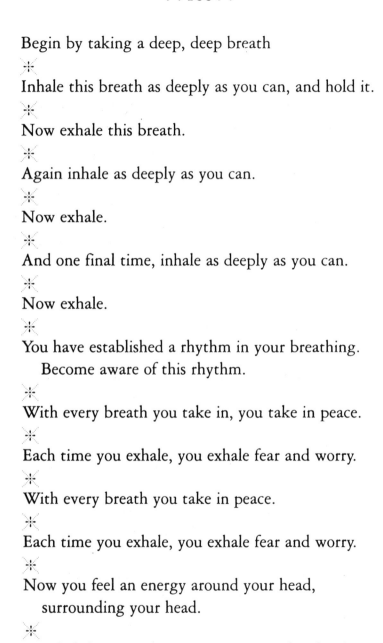

Inhale this breath as deeply as you can, and hold it.

Now exhale this breath.

Again inhale as deeply as you can.

Now exhale.

And one final time, inhale as deeply as you can.

Now exhale.

You have established a rhythm in your breathing.
    Become aware of this rhythm.

With every breath you take in, you take in peace.

Each time you exhale, you exhale fear and worry.

With every breath you take in peace.

Each time you exhale, you exhale fear and worry.

Now you feel an energy around your head,
    surrounding your head.

You feel this energy pouring into your head, relaxing
    your facial muscles.

You relax your facial muscles.

⁜

Your facial muscles relax.

⁜

This energy appears to you as a golden-pink light.

⁜

You feel safe with this light.

⁜

You now feel this energy moving into your face.

⁜

This energy concentrates at a spot on your forehead, between your eyes.

⁜

You feel this energy pouring into a spot on your forehead between your eyes.

⁜

This energy appears to you as a golden-pink light.

⁜

This energy continues to relax all your facial muscles.

⁜

You now feel this energy moving downward and resting on your throat.

⁜

You feel this energy concentrating on your throat.

⁜

You feel this energy pouring into your throat.

⁜

This energy appears to you as a golden-pink light.

⁜

You feel this energy moving down to your heart.

⁜

You feel this energy concentrating on your heart.

❊

You have a feeling of peace and comfort.

❊

You feel a source of love contacting and caressing you.

❊

You bask in this feeling of love and acceptance.

❊

You revel in this feeling of love and acceptance.

❊

You are at peace with this feeling of love and acceptance.

❊

You deserve this feeling of love and acceptance.

❊

This feeling of love and acceptance is your natural state.

❊

This feeling of love and acceptance is your birthright.

❊

You take a moment to enjoy this feeling.

❊

When you are ready, you feel the energy of the golden-
pink light moving down through your torso.

❊

You feel this energy surrounding your vital organs.

❊

You feel this energy concentrating in your stomach.

❊

This energy appears to you as a golden-pink light.

❊

This energy fills you with joy and fulfillment.

You take a moment to enjoy this feeling.

This energy now moves down to your reproductive area.

This area appears as a golden-pink light.

This energy caresses your reproductive area.

This energy releases any subtle guilt that you may feel.

You take a moment to enjoy this energy.

This energy now moves down to the base of your spine.

This area concentrates on the base of your spine.

This energy appears as a golden-pink light.

You feel grounded and safe with this energy.

You take a moment to enjoy this energy.

You now feel this energy moving down your legs to the tips of your toes.

You are now surrounded by a bubble of pink-white light.

You have attracted this bubble of pink-white light to you for peace and protection.

You feel safe in this bubble of light.

You feel at peace in this bubble of light.
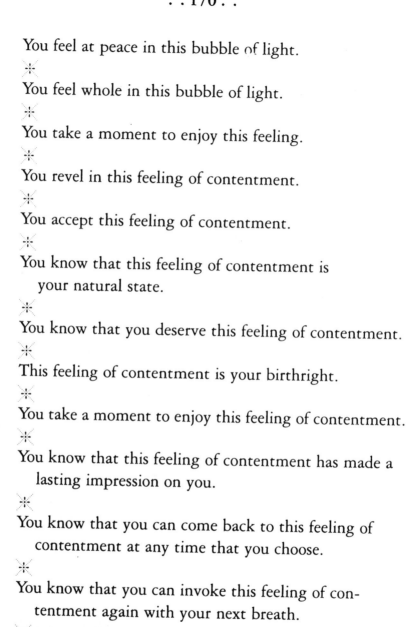
You feel whole in this bubble of light.

You take a moment to enjoy this feeling.

You revel in this feeling of contentment.

You accept this feeling of contentment.

You know that this feeling of contentment is
your natural state.

You know that you deserve this feeling of contentment.

This feeling of contentment is your birthright.

You take a moment to enjoy this feeling of contentment.

You know that this feeling of contentment has made a
lasting impression on you.

You know that you can come back to this feeling of
contentment at any time that you choose.

You know that you can invoke this feeling of contentment again with your next breath.

So when you are ready, you return to the here and now.

When you are ready you become aware of you current

physical space.

⊹

When you are ready, you become aware of your body.

⊹

You wiggle your fingers and your toes.

⊹

When you are ready you come back to the here and now.

⊹

You are now fully present in the here and now, relaxed, refreshed and healed.

Meditation for Building Your Safe Space

Once you feel at peace and relaxed, by using the previous meditation, you can use this meditation to place yourself in your safe space.

You are relaxed and at peace.

⊹

You are content and protected.

⊹

You find yourself at the top of a set of stairs.

⊹

There are 10 stairs in this stairwell.

⊹

You know that you are safe and protected as you take your next steps.

⊹

You step off the ledge onto the first step.

This is step 10.

✳

Step 10 lights up beneath your feet.

✳

This gives you confidence.

✳

You then take your next step.

✳

This is step 9.

✳

Step 9 lights up beneath your feet.

✳

This gives you confidence.

✳

You then take your next step.

✳

This is step 8.

✳

Step 8 lights up beneath your feet.

✳

This gives you confidence.

✳

You then take your next step.

✳

This is step 7.

✳

Step 7 lights up beneath your feet.

✳

This gives you confidence.

✳

You then take your next step.

This is step 6.

✳

Step 6 lights up beneath your feet.

✳

This gives you confidence.

✳

You then take your next step.

✳

This is step 5.

✳

Step 5 lights up beneath your feet.

✳

This gives you confidence.

✳

You then take your next step.

✳

This is step 4.

✳

Step 4 lights up beneath your feet.

✳

This gives you confidence.

✳

You then take your next step.

✳

This is step 3.

✳

Step 3 lights up beneath your feet.

✳

This gives you confidence.

✳

You then take your next step.

This is step 2.

Step 2 lights up beneath your feet.

This gives you confidence.

You then take your next step.

This is step 1.

Step 1 lights up beneath your feet.

This gives you confidence.

There is a well of light at the bottom of this stairwell.

You now turn to the left, and you see a door.

You see light coming from under the door.

You look in the keyhole and see light coming from the keyhole.

You then open the door.

You see a room that is filled with light.

The room is filled with a brilliant white light.

You see a large window in the back of the room.

You see light streaming into this window.

‡

You see a desk and a chair in this room.

‡

This is your desk, and this is your chair.

‡

This room has been prepared especially for you.

‡

The desk and chair face a wall.

‡

On the wall is a large movie screen.

‡

This movie screen will show you scenes of the things that you would like to have in your life.

‡

You take a moment and visualize something that you would like to have and you see it on your movie screen.

‡

You examine the room further.

‡

You see a potter's wheel.

‡

This potters wheel helps you to form the physical objects that you would like.

‡

You go to the potter's wheel and play with it.

‡

You feel the wet, cold, slimy clay between your fingers.

‡

You begin forming an object that you would like.

Before you know it, this object appears fully formed.

✳

Your potter's wheel works.

✳

You look around and see that your room needs to
be decorated.

✳

You pick the furnishings that make you feel comfortable.

✳

You choose floor coverings, wall coverings, or you can
even choose an outside setting.

✳

You can always change your choices.

✳

You look around and you are content in your space.

✳

You look around and you are safe in your space.

✳

You look around and you are powerful in your space.

✳

You then realize that you have the creative power to
create whatever you want in your safe space.

✳

You can create "scenes" that you can experience on
your screen.

✳

You can create objects with you potter's wheel.

✳

You now think of other tools of creation that you would
find useful (such as a printing press for printing
money).

The Power of Prayer...

These additional tools appear before you.

✢

You now make a mental note of how you feel in
your safe space.

✢

You revel in this feeling for a while.

✢

You take a moment to enjoy your safe space.

✢

You know that you can return to your safe space at any
time you choose.

✢

You know that you can take this feeling of safety with
you wherever you go.

✢

So you are now ready to leave this room.

✢

You walk out the door, turning out the light as you leave.

✢

You walk back up the stairs, from Stair 1 to Stair 10,
counting up as you go.

✢

When you get to the top of the landing, you are fully
present in the here and now.

✢

You are fully present in the here and now.

✢

Congratulations, you now have the tools that you need
for any process that you would like to work through in a
prayerful, meditative state. You can combine these guided

meditations with prayer, your own personal ritual, or you can use them alone. They can be an integral part of the process of transformation that you invoke as you walk your path. You can use these tools for a variety of purposes. I will illustrate several ways that they can be used below:

Healing Meditations

You can move to your safe space and visualize your body on your screen. You can then send healing energy in the form of white light to every part of your body, knowing that your body absorbs this healing energy.

You can also visualize any other person or situation on your screen and send healing energy to it in the same way. Although there is always the free will of others to consider, you can always visualize that the other person or the situation absorbs the healing energy. If they do not, it is simply added to the reservoir of healing energy available to you.

If you would like to be a more active participant in this process, you can invoke the healing light into your physical body in the same way that you did in the meditation for peace and protection. In this state, you can surround yourself with light, fill yourself with light and visualize that each and every cell in your body absorbs the light that you send it. You can tell each cell in your body that it is perfect, whole and complete.

You can heal situations from your past in the same way. You can see the situations on your screen, and you can then see them having a different conclusion. If you want to have a more active role in the transformation, you can go in your meditative state, surrounding and filling yourself with white light. You can then move into emotional release and release the energy. You can then envision yourself absorbing the white light of healing. You will know when it is time for you to be more actively involved in the process because you will feel an emotional charge that compels you to release emotionally. When there is no more emotional "charge" left in any situation, then it has nothing left to teach you, and no more power over you. That is when you can truly tell that you have gotten over some event from the past. Also when you have truly gotten over some event from the past, you no longer have to re-create that event for it has brought you into an awareness of the deeper issue, and you have used it to transform this part of your consciousness. This is why the past has no more power over you once you deal with it.

Guided Meditation for Self Acceptance

You can use guided meditations and guided imagery to help you to accept yourself, too. You might begin by going down to your "safe space" and seeing yourself on your screen as a 1 year old child. Concentrate on sending healing energy and loving acceptance to that 1 year old child. Then see yourself at your next birthday and do the same thing. Each time you see yourself as a child, send loving acceptance. Tell the child how wonderful, innocent and perfect he or she is. See yourself embracing the child. Use this technique repeatedly on your 3 year old, then your 4 year old until you reach your current age. This exercise will help you to accept and love yourself more completely and unconditionally. If you need more help with this, John Bradshaw's work on championing and "Healing the Child Within" is an excellent tool.

You might also visualize a treasure chest on your screen. Build an image of opening the treasure chest and finding all kinds of gold and jewels inside. When you look at the jewels, see your reflection in the beauty of their shine. When you see gold coins, see your face on the coins. When you see cash, see your image on the bills. These images will help you to see how precious you really are, and the value that is an intrinsic part of you.

Guided Meditation for Abundance

This last visualization leads right into a guided meditation for abundance. In addition to discovering buried treasure, you can see yourself accepting it. You might also make a note of how you feel at any step in the process. Does it feel awkward for you to discover and accept buried treasure? If so, perhaps there is a part of you that still feels undeserving or unable to manifest your abundance. Continually ask yourself, "how do I feel" and let your feelings guide you into the prayers, visualizations and emotional release necessary to release any blockages that you have to manifesting your own abundance.

One exercise that it might be useful to do is to see the abundance that occurs naturally all around you. You might note the next time you see grass growing out of a crack in the sidewalk, or a tree growing out of a stone on the highway. What this scene tells you is that nature (the universe) is naturally abundant, and GOD, as expressed in nature, must expand and grow and thrive and prosper. This truth might help you to also accept that your prosperity is your divine birthright.

Again the ways that you can use guided meditations and visual imagery are as unlimited as your imagination and the issues that you can overcome. Know always that you will be guided to the imagery that is most useful to you, and protected by the light of GOD as you make these meditations an integral part of your journey.

Chapter Eleven

The Ongoing Journey

The Road Ahead

What you have just begun is a journey that may take days, weeks, months, or even years. This process can be quick and effortless, or it can be as laborious as you choose it to be. That choice is yours. However you choose to take the next steps of your journey, know that the Light of GOD guides you.

What you have read (and hopefully participated in) was a series of concepts and exercises that are designed to help you find your own way to inner peace, abundance, harmony and spiritual growth. Your next steps are to use these concepts, exercises and prayers regularly in your daily life. They are designed to shift your consciousness until the truth in this book BECOMES your consciousness. As this shift occurs, you will create only with the consciousness of truth. Because this consciousness is loving and affirming, you will then create only situations for yourself that are loving and affirming. In truth, you will create the Kingdom of Heaven, here on earth, because you will no longer experience pain or suffering.

You will continually create this heaven by examining your "false-ego" and your reactions to the events that occur in your life. You will recognize how deeply ingrained beliefs (yours and others) have influenced you (many times to your detriment).

You will pray and meditate, so that you become more aware of your "inner cause" (your consciousness) and its "outer effect" (what this consciousness creates in your life). You will then pray for healing, so that your inner cause (your consciousness) shifts. As you continually connect with GOD through this process, you will give GOD permission to transform your consciousness. This connection will increase your awareness of GOD and you will experience the unconditional love of GOD more directly than ever before. As you experience GOD more directly, you will realize that:

GOD loves you
completely and unconditionally

The Universe supports you
completely and unconditionally

You have permission to love yourself
completely and unconditionally

The Ongoing Journey

These "Simple Truths" will pervade your consciousness and eventually will become your consciousness.

However, the next few steps of your journey may not seem much different than the last few steps. You will continue to go to work, play, and fulfill your obligations. However, you will be compelled to examine your motivations, thoughts, beliefs and reactions to your world in a new way. You will filter your experiences through the prism of the new truths that are contained in this book. You will examine your experiences, and the beliefs that you have that create these experiences, and you will take an active role in "un-creating" old experiences and "creating" new experiences. This may take a little work on your part, but your experiences will be excellent tutors for showing you where you are aligned with the Simple Truth, and where you are not. Your experiences will help you build a new consciousness for yourself.

Your new consciousness is like a house – it has a foundation that must be firm, solid and in truth. You are now building that consciousness on that new foundation, and what may be happening to you is that old ideas that were part of your previous consciousness may no longer apply. As a result, your foundation may seem unstable, shaky and creaky.

In truth, the new foundation is being installed, and the old, shaky foundation is being removed. Your consciousness is being remodeled in the same way that a house is remodeled. Just as a remodeling project may expand a house, your new consciousness expands your energy field. During a remodeling project, rooms are expanded, fixtures are being modernized and windows are enlarged to let in more light. The window to your soul is being enlarged to let in more light in the same way. A remodeling project is not pretty. There is dust, dirt and debris. In order for rooms to be enlarged and for larger windows to let in more light, walls must be knocked out. Kitchens and bathrooms must be closed for short periods of time, and this causes inconvenience. In the same way, as your consciousness expands, you may be experiencing some inconvenience.

What you must know is that this inconvenience will not last. There is a contractor managing the whole process. This contractor is GOD. The "workers" are your guardian angels, spiritual guides and teachers. The architect is you. The project is being orchestrated in divine order.

During this period of change, you are being guided, supported and loved. This intricate dance of growth is being choreographed by a choreographer with the utmost qualifications. Have peace, even though the process may seem bewildering at times. Have faith, even though the process may cause you to question your faith. Have no doubt that you are loved, that you are protected, and that this is for your greatest good. Know that the light of GOD will always be with you and will continue to grow within you. Know that you are not alone as you build your new consciousness.

As you build your new consciousness, you will know that you have never left the Garden of GOD's Love. You will know yourself as one of the flowers of this Garden. You can get home again, to the heart of GOD. Getting there requires much courage (you have to examine the scary monsters in the closets of your mind). However, the fact that you have read this book and participated in the exercises shows that you have the courage.

The Ongoing Journey
.. 187 ..

As you continue with this process, have faith in yourself, and have patience every step of the way. Remember to reach out to other like-minded individuals who can support you on your path. Also, always remember that there is light to support you. This light comes from the Heart of GOD, which is your home. Good luck on your Journey.

References

Bradshaw, John. Homecoming: Championing and Healing the Child Within. New York, NY: Bantam Books, 1989.

Errico, Rocco. Let There Be Light (The Seven Keys). Santa Fe, NM: Noohra Foundation, 1996

Foundation For Inner Peace. A Course In Miracles. Tiburon, CA: Foundation For Inner Peace, 1975

Hay, Louise. You Can Heal Your Life. Carson, CA: Hay House, 1984

Ponder, Catherine. Open Your Mind To Prosperity. Marina del Ray, CA: DeVorss and Company, 1971

Ponder, Catherine. The Dynamic Laws of Prayer. Marina del Ray, CA: DeVorss and Company, 1987

Silva, Jose. The Silva Mind Control Method For Getting Help From Your Other Side. New York: Pocket Books, 1989.

Webb, Rev. Jim. Messages From The Masters (The Keys To Enlightened Living.) Merrifield, VA: Prism Publishing, 1999.

Williamson, Marianne. A Return To Love – Reflections On The Principles Of A Course In Miracles, New York, NY: Harper Collins, 1992

Pathways To Inner Peace

If you've found this book helpful to you, and feel that others could benefit by using Pathways, here's how you can order more copies for:

- Your Church or Public Library
- Your Family
- Your Friends
- Other Loved Ones

www.revjimwebb.com
revjimwebb@aol.com
prismpub@aol.com

Contact us to find out about Rev. Webb's Next Book - - *Messages From The Masters (The Keys To Enlightened Living)* or to arrange a seminar, speaking engagement or counseling session with Rev. Webb!